Levi's
Reverse Wave Absorption

Written by
William J. Ryan

Copyright © 2017 William J. Ryan
All rights reserved.

This book may not be reproduced in part or in whole without the written permission of the author. You may write to William J. Ryan at Post Office Box 666, Dade City, Florida 33526

All information, theories and any philosophies or hypotheses should be verified by the reader from outside sources before one takes action to protect oneself from any of the impending dooms that are predicted to come within this book.

All theories and characters in this book (if any) are fictitious and any resemblance to others or actual persons, living or dead, is purely coincidental unless a true name is used and true quotes are used.

OVER BLACK

EXT. APARTMENT COMPLEX - NIGHT

Roll introduction credits over a spliced video of several T.V. and Radio announcers at their desks, doing their shows. We hear the sounds of several announcers over the T.V./Radio waves. After credits are completed we fade to black screen then watch as a scene comes into view. It's late at night in the city and we see a man walking up to an older seven-story apartment complex… he stops and looks up at the building. We hear Levi's voice as he narrates.

Levi looks up at his seven-story older apartment complex which is in the process of being remodeled, and wonders if the hallway to his apartment will be blocked again. He is one of the only tenants left on his floor. It's been a long day and he is tired from working the two part-time jobs he needs to support himself.

His friend Chris keeps telling him to just get a student loan like everyone else, but Levi believes one should pay as he goes. Levi is the first person in his Amish family to go to college, and his tuition is all on scholarship, but he has to pay his own living expenses.

His family is a little more modern than most Amish families, or he wouldn't even be in college. He hurries past all the construction material and empty units, excited because he has finally figured out the formula necessary for the project he's been working on. Once in his apartment, Levi heads to the shower. While showering the phone rings, but he lets the answering machine get it.

The camera focuses in on the phone system as the answering machine answers the phone. We hear Chris' voice…

                           CHRIS   (O.S.)
        Levi… I got the new part. I need to make the
        changes, but it should move things along
        much faster. I think we could be looking at
        moving up your timeline by six months. I
        know you're going to like it. I'll do it
        tonight. See you at five.

We can hear that the shower is still running, so the camera follows the phone line from the recorder down the wall into the socket, through the wall, into the hallway, and out into the main junction box at the base of the apartment complex.

From there, it goes across the street and attaches to another junction box. Then there is a set of cables that enter a phone company van that is parked in front of Levi's apartment. Someone is inside listening to this phone message.

In the dimly lit van we see only the outline of a dark figure from behind as he puts down his headphones and makes some notes in his log. You never see his face as he picks up his cell phone and makes a call.

> **DARK FIGURE**
> They're moving it up by six months. We will need Larry on this one tonight.

CUT TO:

INT. LEVI'S APARTMENT - NIGHT

We can see Levi anxiously looking out his window waiting for Chris. The camera moves in on the window and we watch as a car drives around the back of the complex. It's Chris, in his sister's car.

The camera backs away from the window and we see Levi grab his computer tower and head out the back door to meet Chris in the back parking lot. It seems to be the only place left that's not full of construction material.

Chris and his 105 pound pit bull, named Buford get out of the car. Buford thinks he is a ten-pound poodle, so when they greet one another, Levi is almost knocked down by Buford's love. Chris and Levi exchange the two computer towers. Chris had been storing Levi's old computer as a backup. Chris seemed to be in a hurry to get somewhere.

> **CHRIS**
> Sorry I'm early, but I had a change of plans. I brought your old tower so you can have something to work on while I am upgrading your processor.

> **LEVI**
> That's fine, but make sure you don't mess up any of my work. Your timing is good, though, I won't need it for a few days. I just printed the last of the formula and mailed it to the attorney today.

CHRIS
Don't worry, I won't. It will all be worth it, because your engineering program will be a hundred times faster than it is now. So instead of weeks to estimate one, you can do hundreds in an hour. By the way, I (more) still think your name is lame. RAW… can't you do better?

LEVI
I'm working on it. Thanks for your help. Hey, where is your old van?

CHRIS
It wouldn't start so I had to use my sister's car. She's been out of town and I have to pick her up at the airport. Her boyfriend Jake, missed her and sent her tickets to fly back home for the weekend. They're really in love and he misses her a lot.
She will be coming in on a late flight. If I leave Buford alone for that long he'll howl the whole time, so I was hoping you could take care of him for me and I'll pick him up tomorrow, if that's okay? I can't afford one more complaint or I'm likely to be kicked out of my place.

LEVI
(Petting Buford)
That's fine, Buford's great!

Chris pulls out a black case, which holds his 357 revolver, and hands it to Levi.

CHRIS
I didn't want to leave this in my apartment. Will you hold onto this for me? I certainly don't want to take it to the airport with me. They would probably shoot me on the spot just for having it with me. Everyone is a terrorist nowadays. Be careful with it. It's a real gun and it's loaded.

LEVI
Chris, this is not the first time I've handled a gun. I was raised on a farm, remember, and we went out hunting all the time. So, it's safe with me.

Levi and Chris talk for a while and then Chris remembers his sister. Levi watches as Chris takes off and then he returns to his apartment with Buford leading the way. He hooks at his old computer, thinking he might just use it, but looking at his watch, he doesn't even bother to turn it on, because it's getting late and he decides to crash. He is exhausted from the past week's classes and relieved that he has finally figured out the solution to his problem. He feeds Buford and they crawl into bed together and quickly fell fast asleep.

CUT TO:

INT. APARTMENT COMPLEX - 3 A.M.

We watch as a black shadow appears at Levi's front door. They jimmy the lock and quietly enter the apartment. They quickly spot the computer and walk over to it. All of a sudden, Buford smells something, wakes up and very quietly moves into the room where the computer is located. The shadow is a man, all dressed in black. He begins disassembling the computer. Without making a sound, Buford lunges at the man and rips open his leg. Hearing the scuffle, Levi wakes up and drops to the floor, the gun case is lying next to him, just under the bed.

There is some kind of ruckus going on in the next room and Levi doesn't know what to think. Still trying to wake up, he pulls out the revolver and heads for the doorway. He sees, in the dimly lit room, that the intruder has pulled out his gun and suddenly shoot Buford. In reaction, Levi immediately fires in the direction of the dark shadow.

The shadow returns the gunfire and Levi is shot three times. He doubles over in pain, falls back against the wall, slides down to the floor and becomes motionless. Then Buford makes a deep gurgling sound and takes his last breath. As the last of the air escapes from Buford's lungs, Levi reaches over and strokes his head, but he can't utter a word for the pain he is in. The man reaches for the mike on his shoulder,

                        MAN IN BLACK
        I am hit… I am hit… We need an extraction,
        two of them, and right now! I am hit and
        it's bad!

Buford eyes are fixed on Levi, with his paw pushed into Levi's side. Levi lets out a sigh. Both are now dead.

Minutes later, a U-Haul van pulls up and a crew of men starts removing everything from Levi's apartment, including furniture, his computer, absolutely everything. It is moped and cleaned as though Levi and the dog never existed. Bullet holes are repaired with fast drying patch and painted over as the last of his things are being removed. All signs of damage have disappeared. The scene fades out.

END SCENE

INT. CHRIS' HOME - DAY

A view of a down trodden neighborhood comes onto the screen and focus in on a small house. As the camera moves in closer on the house we see Chris sitting in his kitchen and we hear a phone ring. Chris answers.

(Phone conversation)

CHRIS
Hello? Oh hi Bob…

Bob is a good friend of both Chris and Levi's.

BOB
Something is very wrong. I just went to Levi's apartment and found the door unlocked and the place empty! I mean it's completely spotless. It was never so clean, Chris. Something very strange has happened and all in one night. I don't know what is going on, but we sure need to be careful.

CHRIS
Do you think we should we call the police?

BOB
(Very nervous)
Are you nuts? You don't think burglars did this, do you? If you go to the police, you will be next. I'm gonna lay low. You should to the same.

Extremely uneasy, Chris decides to spend the night at his sister's apartment. Very concerned and confused, all he can think about is Buford and his gun.

CHRIS
I wonder, what could have happened?

Chris' sister agrees to drive Chris back to his apartment, but as a precaution, she parks a block away on the other side of the street. Levi's good computer is still in the trunk of her car.

We watch as Chris begins walking towards his apartment, not noticing the van in the parking lot with two men in it, watching his every move. Chris hurriedly goes up the six flights of stairs and unlocks his front door. He enters his apartment and carefully locks the door behind him.

The first thing he sees is a snapshot on the table of Levi, himself, and Buford. It is a picture recently taken by Bob and he looks hard at the photo trying to see if there is something in it that would explain what has happened. He thinks out loud...

                              CHRIS
                What on earth is going on?

He stares at the picture for quite a while and gently rubs the spot where Buford is as though to stroke his fur. Minutes go by as he stands there trying to understand.

                              CHRIS   (V.O.)
                (Thinking)
                Something is just not right!

While stroking Buford's photo, he hears a sound and quickly looks up and sees a dark figure off to the side in his front window, in the mirror. Then he hears someone unlocking his door trying to come in! He slips all the pictures in his pocket and goes to the back of his apartment and steps out onto the balcony. Next to him, on his left, is another balcony like his with a drain pipe that connects them. He begins to panic.

He tries to think of a way out, looking hard at the other balcony just across from his. He steps out onto the drain pipe, but it is covered with mold and very slippery. Even the balcony railing is wet. He has seen others do this, but he has never tried. Now he must. Just as someone breaks the chain on his door, he tries jumping across onto the balcony next to his and grabs the slippery rail.

CUT TO:

EXT. THE PARKING LOT - DAY

We see a parking lot and focus in on a single car. Its Chris's sister, Roxanne's car. She is bored just sitting in the car all this time and being that she is new in town, she decides to get out, grab her books and go for a walk. She says to herself...

                              ROXANNE
                I need to do some exploring. Maybe I can
                find a quiet spot for some studying.

Roxanne walks a short distance then heads toward Chris's apartment when she hears him calling out her name. She looks up in time to see her brother hanging from the balcony railing, struggling to hold on.

CUT TO:

INT. APARTMENT BUILDING - DAY

The camera pans over to the apartment building across the street, where we see a man and woman sitting on their terrace. They hear Roxanne scream and the man looks up just in time to see someone rushing out onto Chris's balcony. He tells the woman next to him to use her new camera phone to tape the kid's prank. All of a sudden, another man appears and lunges for Chris looking as though he means to push him. They watch as Chris loses his grip, slips and falls.

CUT TO:

EXT. FRONT OF APARTMENT BUILDING - DAY

We watch as Roxanne tosses her books into the air and instinctively runs to try to catch her brother. As if in slow motion, she watches Chris fall six stories to the sidewalk below as she helplessly screams and makes a dive to try to check him. Chris lands right in front of her on the pavement. His skull is shattered, blood and brains splatter everywhere.

Roxanne tries to pick up pieces and put them back in place as she cradles her brother's crushed head in her arms, rocking him, her screams never ceasing. But Chris is dead and she is now covered in blood as she calls out for help, but no one comes. Suddenly what was a busy walkway is now empty, as all the people around disappear. Windows close, curtains are drawn and seemingly, no one is there. Not a single person would come to her aid. Yet there are some do-gooders out there.

The lady across the street, who decided to video the whole thing, pointed to the dark man and yells out…

                      DO-GOODER
        The killer is right there! That's him!

Immediately, her husband calls 911 to report a murder. Another witness spots the van, takes down the tag number, and gives it to the police. Then he calls his favorite radio station and tells them what happened, giving them the tag number and they announce it on the air. Roxanne was in shock. She is taken to the hospital, where she is sedated. The police put out an all-points bulletin for the van, but it can't be found.

That night Roxanne's car is impounded for illegally parking in a one-hour space and is towed to a storage lot in a bad part of town, known for drugs and robberies. But, as such, they have surveillance cameras and a night watchman.

CUT TO:

EXT. IMPOUND LOT - BEFORE DAWN

At 3:20 the morning at the impound lot, three kids break into Roxanne's car and ransack its contents. One tries to take her radio as another goes through her backseat and the other through the trunk. They find and take an overnight bag and Levi's computer, before racing out of the hole in the fence they had just made. They stash their loot and go back into the lot looking for more. This time, the watchman spots them and calls the police. When the dopers hear the sirens, they retreat. Two are apprehended and one gets away.

CUT TO:

INT. FBI BUILDING - MORNING

In the FBI building in Irvine, California, Detective James Cole is sitting at a large table having a meeting with five other people.

                        JAMES
        I need to know what on earth is going on here. Rick, you were in charge of this extraction. Please explain this to us.

                        RICK
           We were confident that this was an HGC (home grown cell) for terrorism. Levi and his friend Chris were working diligently getting information from the internet about extremely large weapons and detonation equipment for bombs, all sorts of very large weapons and detonation devices.
           Because they were moving the timetable up, we felt it was essential to move in and grab their hard drive. All we intended on doing was taking the hard drive, as we have done thousands of times in the past. We had no idea that there was an attack dog on the premises. We knew Levi did not own a gun even though his friend, Chris, did.

                              JAMES
                    (Emphatically)
          How could you miss something like this?
          Didn't you have people watching the
          apartment? That is what we do, you know.

Rick loosens his tie and proceeds to explain what has occurred
over the past twenty-four hours.

                              RICK
          Apparently Chris had parked in the back of
          Levi's building, and we missed seeing Levi
          move the dog and the gun into his apartment.
          We also were expecting them to have a
          meeting at five o'clock and obviously since
          that hadn't happened, we felt it was
          essential that we move in when we did.

                              JAMES
          What did you find on his computer?

Rick says nothing as he looks toward a small man sitting at the
end of the table. One of the other men clears his throat. It's
Robert, the computer expert.

                              ROBERT
          Well, it's not good. My findings can't be
          right. The information we are looking for
          must be in there somewhere. It's very
          puzzling. I have taken all the data apart
          myself and I can't figure out how they are
          hiding the information.

                              JAMES
              I don't need bad news Robert! At some
          point, I have to explain all this. We have
          two dead men and one dead guard dog. We
          broke into a man's apartment and killed him
          and his dog while we were burglarizing his
          place. He had the right to defend himself.
          Don't you see how this will look if the
          media gets wind of it?
              We have major problems here! We don't
          need to look bad again. I will not read
          about having two towers come down on my
          watch. I have had a good career so far and I
          am going to keep it that way. I need to know
          how we are going to straighten this all out!
          What was on that computer?

ROBERT

From what I can tell, this computer hasn't been touched in over six months. If they were working on something, they weren't using that computer. Yet, we could see them and have surveillance pictures of (more) them using it. But the files that I found were not new or current.

RICK

So maybe these guys were a lot smarter than we think.

JAMES
(Unsatisfied)

Well, for the last time… let me ask again… what *was* on the computer?

ROBERT
(Scratching his head)

Well, it looks like he was working on an engineering program for detonating small to large explosions deep inside the earth. It looks like it was intended to take place right around a fault line. Actually, it appears to be the San Andreas Fault.

Apparently, the entire design was to prevent or control earthquakes. From my speed reading the volumes of his work, the basic concept is some type of shock wave absorption system. Those are his words. The idea is to fire off a series of detonations at the very ends of a fault, under cities and densely populated areas, thereby releasing pressure in those spots and sending a shockwave in the opposite direction that the fault normally moves.

The fault line, under the cities would be turned to rubble and virtually disappear at the detonation sites. His theory is that under a large city the ground at each site would be pulverized and the earthquake, which was going to happen anyway, could go ahead and safely happen. At this particular fault, a quake happens every 100-125 years and it has been over a 100 years since the last one. I am thinking the urgency is that the earthquake is due anytime now.

It's a clever idea. This man-made release of pressure would cause the (more) plate shift at a known time. Think of the lives and property that would be saved with these explosions, to force the earthquake to happen at a specific time. The concept would include evacuating the entire area. The military would be called in, ensuring no vandalism. The fuel lines, electricity, gas, and so on, could be turned off and secured with only the addition of the fire departments on stand-by to assist with any fires that may be caused.

Potentially, it could save tens of thousands of lives and hundreds of millions of dollars in property damage. Instead of the earthquake traveling to all ends of the fault lines, including where any cities are, and by the way, where most of the damage would occur, the controlled earthquake would be minimized under the cities and the major damage would take place at the non-detonation sites in remote spots.

The release of this pressure would start the big quake, but the manmade shockwave would be moving in the opposite direction of a normal quake, and the two would meet as it moved into a safer area or one less populated. He has several names for it but I like the name *Reverse Wave Absorption* because it sends a shockwave along the fault line to *absorb* the shockwave coming from the release and meets it head on.

However, let me reiterate, I can find no information newer than six months old in that computer. I am the first one to have gone in in the past six months. No one has at any time since then even logged on to that computer. It just doesn't make sense. It can't be.

JAMES
So, you are telling me that this is not a home grown terrorist cell that we have been monitoring and spending thousands of man hours on all this time! So, watching these people has been just some big mistake? Did you at least get a court order for the phone tapping and break-in?

RICK

Actually, we did not. It just didn't seem necessary. We are in a time of war, sir. When there are terrorists involved, we naturally assume that we have that right.

The President gives us that right, correct? Now, to move on, there must be another computer someplace. How could he have a computer that hadn't been used for six months? There must be something we missed. We have all his personal property and there is no laptop, no extra disks, nothing. It doesn't add up. We've missed something.

JAMES

I have a meeting in Washington and I have to explain to them how all this happened. So far, you are telling me it's limited to this one incident.

RICK

Oh, you don't have to worry sir. It is contained. We believe we have every end sewed up.

JAMES
(Laughing)

You have every end sewed up? Are you nuts?! There are innocent people dead, blood splattered all over the place, and you are telling me you have it cleaned up! This is a major problem, and I am six months away from retirement.

If you think for one second that I am going to lose my pension and leave the FBI in disgrace, you are one hundred percent wrong! I could possibly even go to jail! You guys have bungled this, and if anyone is going down, it's you, not me. So I suggest you all get together and figure out how to dress this up!

RICK
(Respectfully)
Yes sir!

James stands up.

                    JAMES
          Okay then, we are going to meet this
          afternoon. I leave for Washington tomorrow
          morning and I want a good plan. You guys put
          your heads together and use whatever working
          brain cells you have left to come up with
          something.

CUT TO:

INT. CONFERENCE ROOM, FBI HEADQUARTERS - 2 P.M.

James and five other men begin a meeting in the conference room to find out what to do about their mistake.

                    JAMES
          Well, I hope you all have good news for me.
          I want to know how we are going to handle
          this.

                    RICK
            We do have some explanations. The first
          thing we'll say is that Chris' death, whose
          fall was seen by witnesses, was an accident.
          We can't cover this one up, but we have
          leaked it out on the street that it was a
          college prank. The extraction of Levi and
          the dog is a totally different matter
          however. No one has reported him missing so
          we still have time to come up with
          something.
            A couple of ideas - one, he could have
          left to go live with a girlfriend. Two, he
          died of a drug overdose, or three, he
          couldn't handle the workload of school and
          went back home. Or, maybe he killed himself.
          The good news is, we still have some time.

The room goes deadly quiet. James taps his fingers on the desk, while he glares at Rick, and starts to turn red as the veins pop out on the side of his neck.

                    JAMES
          That is not exactly what I call good news,
          but it is some progress since this morning.
          So I still have time, do I? That's nice to
          know. Somehow, I have to explain this to
          Washington, and it is still not good. Now,
          uh, does anyone have an update on Larry?

RICK
(Clearing his throat)
It is not good sir. Larry passed away at eleven o'clock this morning.

JAMES
(Trying to stay calm)
So let me get this straight! We burglarized a college kid's apartment because we had wrong information and killed him and his guard dog. Then we are involved in a second incident, in which another innocent kid falls to his death trying to get away from us.

By the way, I also understand that both were pretty bright students too, not loser dopers. From what we have found out so far, they were non-alcoholic, non-drug users, and by the way, Levi didn't even have a girlfriend. He was strictly there to hit the books. Now, to top it off, we have lost one of our best extraction people, Larry! I've known him for over fifteen years. How he let you talk him into doing this job is beyond me! He really must have let his guard down. And here's another thing...
(Loudly)
Apparently, the information that these kids were working on seems not only harmless, but could be quite beneficial. As you can see, this is all not good. I want to know how we got it so wrong. I need to know! Somebody better get me some answers. I am leaving first thing in the morning and I don't like early morning flights, so we need this ironed out before I go.

RICK
We are trying to find out more information on Chris, the one that fell. He had a sister, but she has been heavily sedated ever since the accident and we are unable to talk to her. They had no other living family that we know of.

JAMES
(Angrier than ever)
So, let's review one more time. We wire tapped the phone and broke into a home without a warrant. We killed a guard (more)

dog, guarding the property. We killed a student defending his home from an intruder. Another student, running from a home invader, falls to his death.

The local police are looking for his killer. In addition, one of our best agents, attempting to retrieve some needed documentation, died because you did not inform him of a gun and a guard dog. Are we all clear?

James grabs his briefcase and storms out of the office without saying another word.

CUT TO:

INT. AIRPLANE – BEFORE DAWN

The scene is inside an airport terminal, where we see James boarding the red-eye flight to DC. James takes his seat on the plane and begins reviewing his report, but he keeps returning to the drawing made by Levi. Images of a newspaper headline with his photograph keep flashing through his mind. We see a flash of a newspaper headline that reads:

> **California FBI director caught in double murder cover up… FBI director arrested…Innocent college student's victims of bungled investigation… 5 indictments.**

James rubs his forehead and begins thinking of his lakefront home, his wife, his children, and his grandchildren. What would they think if he was arrested? There would be so much shame to endure. Suicide passes through his mind.

               JAMES
    (Mumbles to himself)
I can't let this happen to them. I won't put them through that. What if we can't fix this? I must find a way… I must find a way!

We watch as the plane touches down at its destination. Then James disembarks and heads out of the airport to a waiting car.

CUT TO:

INT. OUTER OFFICE OF FBI HEADQUARTERS – MORNING

James arrives at the FBI Washington Headquarters for his seven a.m. meeting. Upon his arrival, he finds that his meeting is postponed until eight a.m. and he has to wait. He is sitting in an outer office when a gentlemen walks in. It is Fred, assistant to Mr. Bates, and head of the FBI. He walks up to James…

FRED
I understand we have a problem?

JAMES
Yes sir.

FRED
Why don't we go in my office and discuss it?

JAMES
I will only speak to Director Bates.

FRED
It must be something pretty big, or is it that bad? You guys must have really screwed up something big. You can tell me. It may help to present it in a better light.

JAMES
I will only speak to Bates in private.

FRED
If it is that big, maybe those idiots at Homeland Security should be informed.

JAMES
No one needs to be informed of anything until I speak to Director Bates. You got that?

Fred speaks into an intercom going into the inner office…

FRED
Sir, Mr. Cole is here and I think we have a bigger problem than we thought.

Bates responds on the intercom…

BATES
Then by all means, send him in.

JAMES
(To Fred he walks by)
I will let Bates explain things to you. As I said, I will only speak to him.

FRED

If this is another screw up… you know he's not going down with you. I won't let you trash this office again.

JAMES

Don't worry. I know whose heads are going to roll.

FRED

That's good.

James walks into the Director's office and closes the door. After a brief greeting and handshake, James begins to explain everything that has happened to Bates. When done both Bates and James walk out of the office chatting…

BATES

If this thing turns ugly, I'm not going down with anyone, I tell you that. You need to make sure everything is taken care of. Even if you need a fall guy… let me know. We will find someone.

JAMES

Oh, I will keep you informed, no matter what. I promise you, it will be taken care of and I already have my fall guy in the wings.

BATES

Good, then neither of us have a problem, do we… Let me speak with the President. Would you mind waiting in the outer office for a while?

JAMES

No not at all.

Once back in his office, Bates makes a call to the office of the President of the United States.

BATES

I would like to make an appointment for a private meeting with the President.

SECRETARY

Would 2 P.M. this afternoon be good for you?

BATES
Perfect! Thank you.

CUT TO:

INT. OVAL OFFICE - 2:15 P.M.

Bates meets with the President and explains how a suspected terrorist cell was investigated and in the process of preserving our way of life, apparently a few innocent people got hurt.

BATES
Mr. President. Since 9/11, when they tried to destroy us and our way of life, you know how hard we have all been working. You said terrorists must be stopped at all costs, that innocent people are going to be hurt, but we have to do what we have to do.

PRESIDENT
I understand. Yes, I want them stopped at all costs!

BATES
I was sure you would understand. Apparently, during the investigation one of our agents shot and killed a guard dog and a suspect. He was shot in the process and died from his wounds. Another suspect fell to his death while trying to avoid being questioned.
It seems that our agents got over zealous and misinterpreted what these young men were doing. It turns out that they had devised a plan to save lives. They called it the "*Reverse Wave Absorption*."

PRESIDENT
(Showing no concern)
So tell me again about the *Reverse Wave Absorption* idea. Was that to be used with nuclear weapons?

BATES
Not specifically. The young student was trying to access state-of-the-art military armaments, such as the ones used in Afghanistan, to blow up those caves. His notes state clearly that no nuclear arms are to be used. For one thing, it would (more)

destroy the water table. I can assure you that we are doing our best at damage control.

PRESIDENT

Oh, I am not worried about that. After all, I am the President. I know you're controlling the damage, or you will. This administration is not going to look bad because of the FBI's bungling of another situation.

You are going to take care of this, I'm not worried. But leave me the information. I want to see the entire report on what we understand and know about this earthquake control thing. That is what we are talking about here… right?

BATES

Yes sir. Earthquakes and volcanoes, with the right armaments, situations like Mount St. Helen, where sixty-three people were killed, could be prevented. We could figure out exactly how to remove the entire top off that volcano. The detonations are to be all done at the same time and the pressure is released simultaneously, over a large area. Rather than a small area, in one gigantic burst.

It is like removing the bottom of a champagne bottle as opposed to the top. Once you release all the pressure, there won't be a big explosion miles into the atmosphere, but one contained safely in a small area. Also, we control the moment it will happen, so that no one should get killed and property damage is minimized.

The President leans forward, his hand cradling his chin.

PRESIDENT

You realize the significance of what you are saying, don't you? This could give my reputation a real boost. Make sure nobody leaks this information. We need an expert on seismology and volcanoes and I need to review that report at once.

BATES

Yes, Mr. President, I will get right on it.

Bates puts a copy of the report entitled *Levi's Reverse Wave Absorption* on the President's desk.

The President watches Bates leave and a he begins to grin broadly. He scratches out the word *Levi* and replaces it with *Project*. Then sits back and rubs his palms together, thinking that his dad would be so proud.

With the meeting over, Bates returns to speak with James. James is anxious and Bates can tell that he is by how white his knuckles are as he grasps the arms of the chair.

JAMES
How did it go?

BATES
Well, I omitted a few small problems, which I figure you will take care of and the President said to tell you, 'good job.'

JAMES
You omitted a few things?

BATES
Oh, he understands the situation and frankly, he doesn't care. He said you did a good job and that the information you got was extremely valuable. I will need a full updated report as soon as possible for a meeting tomorrow morning. I will also need a complete overview of this plan, this *Reverse Wave Absorption* idea. Do you understand?

I would suggest you have it here by six a.m. on my desk and don't worry about things, James. He said good job, so pass that on to your men. By the way, I am sorry to hear about Larry. He was a good man. Somebody sent him into that trap. Somebody screwed up bad and got him killed. The real crime is no one will ever pay for his wasted life.

I hope nothing like this happens again. You are so near retirement, maybe it's time you looked at early retirement, James. I think you should think about that.

JAMES
Yes sir, I have thought about that and I think it is sound advice.

                    BATES
    It's always good to leave on a high note. I
    know Larry had no family but us. You are
    taking care of his arrangements, aren't you?

                    JAMES
    Oh, yes sir. Do you want me to call you on
    the details?

                    BATES
    Of course!

CUT TO:

INT. THE WHITE HOUSE - DAY

The President wastes no time in calling an old friend; an armament manufacturer who has been very helpful in the past with regards to campaign contributions.

                    PRESIDENT
    Jack, I think you should know that I've got
    something for you.

                    JACK
    Well good! I am always happy to hear from
    you and I love good news from our President.
    How I can help you Mr. President?

                    PRESIDENT
    Well, something has come up that I think you
    will be very interested in.

                    JACK
    Yes, I want to hear more. When would you
    like to meet?

                    PRESIDENT
    I should have all the information by
    tomorrow in a seven a.m. meeting, so how
    about ten o'clock tomorrow morning in my
    office?

                    JACK
    Yes sir, Mr. President, I will be there.

The President sits back in his chair and spins it in a circle. He has a great big smile on his face just like a kid in front of the Christmas tree. He arranges to have the report Bates left delivered to a seismologist and a volcanologist. Then he is busy looking out the window plotting how to use this information to help boost his approval rating and preserve his reputation as the best president ever, because he saved the United States from another disaster. He can't remember being so happy.

CUT TO:

INT. THE OVAL OFFICE - 6:30 AM

We see the President walking down the hall, heading to the Oval Office and mentally preparing for his 7 A.M meeting. As he arrives at his office, he sees Jack sitting in the hall outside of his office door.

> **PRESIDENT**
> Well Jack, you're here kind of early

> **JACK**
> The art of being on time often accompanies being early, Mr. President.

> **PRESIDENT**
> Yes, it does. I have that important meeting at seven o'clock and as a matter of fact, I think you should sit in on it, just to listen. This is all top secret, you understand.

> **JACK**
> Yes, Mr. President, I understand.

> **PRESIDENT**
> I think you're going to be very happy with what you hear. This is going to make us quite a bit of money.

> **JACK**
> I am sure it will be good for the both of us and the country.

They both laugh as the President leads Jack into the oval office, patting him on the back.

> **PRESIDENT**
> I like the way you think, Jack. I have to take care of my friends now, don't I? After all, they helped me get my position. Now you understand, I am helping to pay you back.

JACK

Mr. President, I am just glad to help the country in any way that I can. I have always been very grateful and it's been a profitable relationship for all of us.

PRESIDENT

No doubt about it, Jack.

The meeting was delayed until eight a.m. because Jack and the President are too busy talking over old times. Finally, the meeting begins. Those present are Bates, the head of the FBI, and Steve, a seismologist, from the Smithsonian. Also present is Jack, sitting quietly.

PRESIDENT

I assume you both had time to review everything and can give me an analysis of this absorption thing.

BATES

Yes Sir, I have studied it most of the night.

PRESIDENT

Good, good, I want your opinion. What do you think of this?

BATES

Well, remember, I am not an expert. However, on the surface, if done properly, it makes a lot of sense. As we speak, I am having computer models made to test the idea.

PRESIDENT
(Turns to the seismologist)
What is your opinion on this? Please keep it in laymen's terms, simple and short.

STEVE
(Looking surprised)
   Alright Mr. President… I think we haven't even begun to comprehend the incredible requirements of drilling into the earth and setting off explosives. The effort that would be necessary would cost billions of dollars. Besides the enormous expense, it also would be a very time consuming endeavor and we have no comprehension of the real outcome. This is bigger than ten (more)

Hoover Dams and I estimate the whole project would take anywhere from ten to twenty years.

Certainly, this is not something that could be done in the short term. It is complicated and would require a considerable amount of engineering expertise before you drill your first hole. When you release these kinds of forces, you have to be ready for the outcome. If you *cause* it to happen, you are even more liable. Before you open this up and release the type of extreme pressure we're talking about, a great deal of consideration must be taken.

PRESIDENT
So, what you are saying is that it would be an enormous undertaking, take an intense amount of drilling, and require very sophisticated armaments for detonation.

STEVE
And timing… The timing sequence is extremely relevant to the position of the fault. If you are going to release the pressure at the far end, it all must be done in sequential order so that the wave is sufficiently distant from any population before the main fault is released and they meet.

PRESIDENT
(Sits back and spins in his chair)
So, couldn't we speed things up if we drilled fewer holes and used bigger bombs? That would take care of the time thing, right?

Thank you both for putting so much time in on this. If I need any further assistance I will contact you.

STEVE
Mr. President, I…

BATES
(Rushing Steve out the door)
The President has a busy day Steve.

After Bates and Steve leave, the President turns to his friend Jack.

                    PRESIDENT
I'm letting you in on all this to repay you for all your support and campaign contributions. There's a lot of money to be made.

                    JACK
I thank you, sir, but how will we get the money to pay for all this?

                    PRESIDENT
Oh there's plenty of money. You don't have to worry about that. This is America. If we need more money we just print it. All you need to worry about is spending it. Now, I need you to start this project immediately.

                    JACK
      (Smiles and salutes)
Yes sir. Consider it done!

They shake hands heartily, and then Jack steps out of the office and hurries to talk to Steve.

                    JACK
Steve, before you go, let me ask you, how deep do these fissures or plates run into the earth?

                    STEVE
Oh, they go all the way into the core of the earth.

                    JACK
So it is safe to say, five hundred or a thousand miles?

Steve tries to hold back his look of shock as to how little this man knows and responds in a professional manner.

                    STEVE
Yes, well probably not that deep, and some faults run right on the surface. So they could run at any level.

                    JACK
Good. Thank you. I think that answers my question.

Jack returns to the President's office and asks him...

                              JACK
           Do you want me to involve Steve in this?

The president leans back in his chair, looks out the window.

                            PRESIDENT
    Steve? God, no! I can't stand people like that. They're the 'can't do' people of the world. Nothing would ever get (more) done if you listened to people like him. What would we have done in World War II if we had had people like that? Oh, we can't build a bomber. It takes twenty years to design it to be safe. I say, build it. Put it up in the air and worry about the clean-up later.
    We have to get the job done and there isn't a lot of time to do it, so toss the worry warts out the window and surround yourself with 'can do' people. We should move on this and move fast. From the sound of it, we don't have a lot of time. So, do your research, but do it quickly. Get a lot of people on it and I will get the funding headed your way.

END SCENE

INT. AIRPLANE - SATURDAY MORNING, MAY 29th

James had stayed overnight in Washington to insure the report was finished on time and now is on a plane heading back to California. He sits quietly thinking about the people on this case.

There's Rick, the man in charge, headstrong, and kind of a loose cannon. He's ambitious and that could make him dangerous. Even though he is somewhat difficult to control, most of the time James knows he is right. He is a good man, but this is a job that is going to require something not found in Rick: dedication at any cost. Then, there is Martin, assistant to Rick.

Martin is definitely more gullible. He can control him easier, and tell him to do the job for the good of the country and he will. He understands. Rick is a different story. He leans back in his window seat and stares at the dark sky outside and sighs.

                JAMES (V.O.)
      (Thinking to himself)
  I have known Rick since we were kids.

The plane goes through a thunderstorm that occasionally lights up the clouds. James thinks once again,

                JAMES (V.O.)
      (Thinking)
  If I screw this up what's going to happen? The only thing left to do would be to take my own life. How? Hanging? Jumping off a bridge? Shooting myself through the pituitary? That's the best way - it's over in a tenth of a second.

James makes a phone call.

                JAMES
  I want an eleven o'clock meeting tonight, and make sure Rick and Martin are there.

James arrives at the California office of the FBI jet-lagged, but determined. Rick the project manager and Martin, his assistant, are waiting outside his office.

                JAMES
  Good, I am glad you are both here, come inside my office.

As they all sit down James goes on…

                    JAMES
I have great news!

Rick and Martin look at each other kind of surprised.

                    JAMES
The President was extremely pleased with my report, and the outcome is better than we had hoped for. Also, Bates said to tell you, 'Congratulations, job well done.' Promotions are coming, I can smell it and this is good for all of us.

                    RICK
          (An angry look on his face)
What do you mean this is good for all of us? It doesn't make any sense, how did that happen?

                    JAMES
Well, it's simple. The President appreciates the work and dedication in finding out about this loosely tied home-grown terrorist group and he is very pleased.

                    RICK
Terrorist group… Is *that* what we are going to call this?

                    JAMES
Well, we are not sure exactly how we are going to do this yet, but I like the ring of it.

                    RICK
          (Outraged)
You can't do that! These two boys were no home-grown terrorist group and you know it! It doesn't make any good sense. I told you before. I won't be part of it! You should know that by now. We have known each other since we were kids. I won't do it! I won't have any part of the destruction of these two boys' reputations just to save my own skin!

At that point, James turns to Martin…

JAMES

Would you mind stepping out, I really need to talk to Rick alone.

RICK

He doesn't need to leave. He can hear what you have to say.

JAMES

Martin, please leave the room for a few moments.

Martin gets up and leaves the room.

RICK
(Infuriated)
What makes you think you are going to make me cover this thing up and lie about what's happened here?

JAMES
(Leans back in his chair)
Well, I don't think, I *know* you will. You *will* clean it up! It's not the first time you've had to do this, so climb off your high horse.

RICK

Don't hand me that! There have never been other situations like this one and I have never done that. I have sat back and kept my mouth shut before, but I have never participated in one of your cover-ups, while others in this organization have.
(Looking hard at James)
You know when we were kids your old man never did trust you. He never understood what made you so ambitious and willing to bend the rules. Your dad was a good cop for his whole life.

JAMES

What do you really know about my dad? He wasn't an open person.

RICK

He wasn't open with you, but he was with me.

JAMES

I don't believe it! He never opened up to anybody! He would come home at night and just sit in his chair and not say a word.

RICK

He trusted me and took me into his confidence. You know he was in Dallas that day and he shared things with me.

JAMES

Yeah… sure! I know he never talked about that, not to anyone.

RICK

He talked about it to me and I will tell you something else. Before he passed on, he gave me a case full of evidence that he had compiled over the years, regarding John's assassination. It's still safe and intact in his old black valise.

JAMES
(Bothered by the conversation)
Don't start this. I don't want to hear this junk.

Rick wouldn't let up…

RICK

That's the reason he wouldn't talk to you, because you are so closed minded. You wouldn't look and you wouldn't listen. He knew better, but the point is, I've got the evidence and it is strong, powerful and distinctively clear that there was a major cover up.

You know what? Maybe it is time to come out with it. Maybe I need to just dig it out and go to the media. I can tell them everything, or better yet, I can stop this foolishness and finish writing my book.

JAMES

That would really be a dumb mistake! First off, you would go down for this mess we're in now, not anybody else. I would make sure you would hang. Secondly, I don't believe there really is a black case. I have heard rumors of it, but I don't believe it. (more)

My old man was pretty good, but he wasn't that sharp, so I just don't believe it.

RICK
(Stands up)
Well, I guess we are at an impasse. It is time I give all this serious consideration.

JAMES
You can't leave. We have a lot of work to do. I don't need you taking off thinking about anything! You have a job to do here and you won't risk everything over this. You're not that kind of a man. You never were.

RICK
(Speaking firmly)
I *am* leaving and I think you already know what I am going to do!

JAMES
(Stands up)
It would be the biggest mistake of your life.

RICK
Not doing anything would be the biggest mistake of my life. And there is one more thing you should consider, I have seven independent head agents working on more than one hundred deferent cases right now. Martin was in charge of this one, so we both know who bungled this and it was not me.
As his supervisor I reported it to you, so you are going to leave me out of this one. You two can do whatever you want, but like I said, I'm out of the loop on this one. And don't think I am quitting. You're not going to get rid of me that easily. Oh, yeah, there is one more thing.
(Pulling a small recorder from his coat pocket)
Like I said, nothing is going to happen to me, or this whole thing will end up like the Baby Aisenberg case in Tampa. And you don't want that.

With that Rick turns around and walks out.

JAMES
(Shouts)
If you just quit, you need to give me your badge.

RICK
(Shouts back)
I just told you, I didn't quit, I'm just going home. If you have a problem with me, let's bring it before the review board, and see what they have to say.

Rick smiles, and keeps walking out of the main office very slowly with all eyes on his back. Martin watches it all, wide-eyed, and then stands up.

JAMES
Come on in, Martin. I am now the new project manager of this mission and it's in crisis. Action must be taken immediately.

Martin snaps to attention. James thinks that Martin must be the best yes-man in the FBI.

MARTIN
Yes sir! What do you need me to do?

JAMES
The first thing I need you to do is gather up all Levi's belongings, put them in a truck and take them to Arizona. When you get out in the desert, you set everything on fire, including the body, and burn it.
Whatever he had - car, clothes, his computer - wait, not his computer, I don't want to lose his computer. We aren't finished with it yet. Burn everything else, so there isn't one thing left. Got it?

MARTIN
Yes, sir! Are you sure this is what we need to do?

JAMES
You don't' understand, this comes all the way from the top, and it is not going anywhere else.

MARTIN
I understand.

JAMES

Now, tomorrow morning you are going to have a press conference and we will be asking the public if they have any information that could help with Levi's disappearance.

Make up a story about somebody having been seen in the area that night and paint a blurry picture of a car driving by. Those are the greatest misinformation things to give the news. And see if we can get this on "America's Most Wanted."

MARTIN

But, sir, we know where he is.

JAMES

Of course we do. This is a cover up you idiot! Then, let the police know we are helping them as much as we can. We are going to plea to the public for help in this horrible, horrible crime. If you get any information on what he was up to or what was going on, let me see the press release before you send it out.

MARTIN

Yes, sir, I will start on it right now, I will get his stuff together.

JAMES

Don't forget his body!

MARTIN

I won't, I will make sure we take it.

JAMES

One more thing Martin, you report only to me. You do nothing without first talking to me. Got it? Call me when you get in the Arizona desert, before you start the fire, just in case something has changed. Rick is no longer your supervisor. You only report to me on this case.

James knows that now Levi's body will be crossing the state line, they are definitely involved. He smiles to himself realizing that this is a major cover-up and he knows exactly what to do. Once more Rick was right, not wanting it to end up like Tampa and the "Baby Sabrina" disappearance. We certainly all learned how to do our jobs better from that experience.

Martin leaves the office with all the boxes in tow. With Martin gone, James picks up the phone, turns in his chair and faces the window. From outside the building looking in, you can see James talking on the phone, but you can't hear what he is saying.

Cars are driving by in the street below and only the usual city traffic noises can be heard. There is honking and a siren blaring in the distance. A soft night breeze blows and bends the limbs of a nearby tree. You can read James' lips and know what he is saying into the phone…

JAMES
I need Rick, dead, TONIGHT. I called you about it before and he is en route now. You know his way home. It must be taken care of tonight.

Then he begins to laugh and enjoy talking to this person. He finally ends his conversation with a big smile of satisfaction on his face and hangs up the phone.

CUT TO:

EXT. PARKING LOT - NIGHT

Rick stops at a local store and picks up a disposable cell phone. He activates it and calls his wife Janet. He has warned her that if something big ever came up he would call her on her secondary phone and on that number only, so to always keep it near. In his home, the second phone rings and his wife rushes to pick it up.

JANET
(Nervously)
Rick, are you okay?

RICK
Yes, but I am afraid it's finally happened.

His wife worriedly begins to ask him questions.

RICK
No, don't say anything in the house. I don't trust anyone at this point and neither should you. I want you to remember if anything should happen you know who to contact, you know where to go, right?

> **JANET**
> I have been dreading this. But, when you get here we will do what we have to do and we will do it together.
>
> **RICK**
> Fine, just remember what I said.

Here we start to see several scenes. We are switching back and forth, from scene to scene.

Rick hangs up the phone and starts to drive. It is about an hour's drive to get home. Along the way a speeding car begins darting in and out of traffic, racing past everyone, even passing on the shoulder. The car is an ex-state police car still bearing the crudely painted over sticker residue. It pulls up even with Rick's car and slows down to match his speed and the driver raises an Uzi and fires. Hundreds of bullets hit Rick's car causing him to lose control and careen off the side of the road into the thick brush. But he is still alive.

A student driver was right behind Rick's car at the time of the shooting and it so happens that his parents had installed a recorder on the mirror to monitor his driving. He gave chase to the shooter but had to stop when the police pulled him over.

Meanwhile, Rick is in his car concealed in the brush with his eyes closed taking stock. First he checks the movement of his hands, arms and shoulders, so far… so good. He reaches up to brush the glass from his eyes and mouth and in the dark he checks for any blood and he could find none. He looks around the car to find all the glass was shattered. He smiles, thinking that his training has paid off.

He had spotted that car driving erratically and coming up behind him. When it had slowed down and pulled up next to him he had seen the muzzle of the gun pop up and he ducked down and swerved just in time.

Meanwhile, the student driver shows the police his video camera tape and gives him a description of the car. The officer calls it in and finds that a TV news traffic chopper is in the area reporting and it has spotted the unusual driving of two cars. So when the shooting is reported, the chopper stays with the alleged shooter's car.

Rick climbs out of the car and calls his wife. When she answers, he says one word, "NOW!" and hangs up the phone. Then he smells gasoline and realizes his gas tank is leaking. He walks around to the back of the car and sees something has caught it on fire.

                              RICK
                    That should help them find the car. Let's
                    see them hide this.

At this point, Rick takes off into the woods. The shooter's car is now live on the local news, showing the police chase. The gunman is headed downtown and side streets are blocked off as he goes toward the docks. Finally, at a speed of over one hundred miles per hour he drives over the end of a pier and pierces the upper deck of a yacht in the bay. This only helps to slow down the car before it hits the water and quickly sinks to the bottom.

Back at Rick's car, the fire rapidly rages. Rick must find a safe place to go, because the wind has changed directions and now the fire is spreading dangerously toward him. Just in time, he finds a culvert running under the road and he slips down inside it.

By now, the fire now is moving at over sixty miles an hour and it races by him with all the fury of a freight train. It sucks out the air in the culvert replacing it with smoke. He pulls his coat over his head and lays flat on the ground.

A little while later, Janet is watching the whole fire storm story on the late breaking news as she packs some bags. Their daughter, Katy, wakes up and comes out to be comforted and Janet turns down the sound. Katy was a conjoined twin. Her sister Sara was attached to her right side and when she became very ill not too long ago, they had to separate them to save one. Katy now carries a doll with her on that same side all the time.

Katy asks her mother what is going on. Janet tells her they are going on a trip and they're going to play a game with daddy. Katy likes games. She hopes this will help take her mind off the recent loss of her sister and tries to make it sound like a lot of fun.

CUT TO:

INT. FBI OFFICES - NIGHT

It's past midnight and James is sitting in his office alone waiting for the call that told him that his guy was successful when he falls asleep, unaware of the events that were unwinding. Suddenly the phone rings, but it's not the call he's expecting, it's the police. They have traced the tag number of the burning car to the FBI.

By the time more information works its way through the bowels of the FBI, its four thirty a.m. and James gets another call.

                         ANONOMOUS
          I'm sorry to disturb you sir, but it was Rick's car. The car is full of bullet holes and it burst into flames starting a major wild fire. The local police have the car and all the news channels are showing pictures of it all over the air. The fire is now reported to be burning out of control with over thirty homes being taken out. A major evacuation has been ordered. If you look out your window, sir, you can see the flames from where we are and coming right at us.

James quickly looks out the window. He is envisioning the charred body of his friend in a closed casket, the news headlines, and the investigation. His only reaction is to pee his pants.

CUT TO:

INT. RICK'S HOME - MORNING

The next morning, Janet, knows she must play the part of not knowing what is going on. She calls Rick's office speaking to James' assistant,

"Rick never came home last night, I'm afraid something bad has happened. He's not answering his phone, nobody I've talked to has seen him, and nobody knows what's going on. I've seen your people on TV. I am watching the news. The FBI is talking about needing help solving some crime. What is going on?"

The assistant tells her that Martin is the lead investigator in the crime she is referring to, and it's in that moment Janet realizes what has happened. He says that Martin is out on another case but he will get him to call her when he has news.

In fact, Martin is unavailable because he is in the middle of an interrogation. The night before, Martin had had Roxanne picked up and taken to an undisclosed location for intense questioning because they consider her to be part of the terrorist cell. They began using the water board and Martin justified his actions by telling his men that the President approves it in times of war, "And by god, we are in war!"

Janet quickly ends the conversation, quietly turns to her daughter and tells her in whispers to pack a few things for her dad. The daughter already knows and has been prepared.

Soon, a black van and two black government sedans pull up in front of their house and six men dressed in dark suits get out. They talk for a moment and two of them come up to the front door, knock and announce that it's the FBI. Janet opens the door and they tell her something has happened to her husband, that he must have fallen asleep at the wheel.

They say they must retrieve his files and the case paperwork he was working on. Janet reaches down and pulls her daughter closer and presses her tight against her, stepping aside. The men briskly walk past them through the front door. Inside, they coldly and methodically begin their search. They go through drawers, filing cabinets, closets and they take what they want.

They load up his desk, his furniture, his cabinets, pictures, and personal belongings from his office. They march out the door like robots carrying everything that was tied to her husband. She says nothing. Once they are out in the van and start the vehicles, Katy writes a note on a piece of paper and hands it to her mother and it reads…

Is it okay to talk now?

Janet writes…

No.

Janet takes the pencil and points to the phone, indicating that they are bugged.

Janet looks out the window and sees that one black car remains with two dark figures sitting in it. She casually takes her daughter's hand and they go out to the driveway and hop in their minivan as if they are going off to run some errands, no big deal. She drives to town down Main Street, with the black car tailing her.

They do some grocery shopping and pick up the dry cleaning, waiting for the right moment. Finally, they give the FBI men the slip. As they walk through a department store at the mall, Janet spots someone getting out of a cab by one of the exits. They quickly grab that cab and take off in the opposite direction.

They go to the taxicab's main office to make some arrangements. Then Janet, with some shopping bags and Katy in tow, return to the same mall and walk back through the same department store as though nothing has happened. Meanwhile, the FBI men have been looking all over for her. She takes her time looking at dresses, trying on some shoes, and so on, until they finally get back in their minivan and take off for home.

END SCENE

INT. KENTUCKY, SHERIFF'S OFFICE - DAY

Notification of Chris's death is slow getting to his family. When it finally comes to the desk of the local sheriff, in Chris' Kentucky hometown, he goes out and tells the family.

Chris had two brothers, Elwood and Lamar, two big boys from muleskinner backgrounds. After being told of their brother's death, they tell Roxanne's fiancé, Jake that they are going to California to find out what happened to their brother.

> **JAKE**
> Not without me, you're not.

In size, Jake makes Elwood and Lamar look sickly. They decide to take Jake's car. His father is a moonshiner and his car is the fastest in the county, made to outrun the G-men. They still have no word of what has happened to Roxanne and Jake is going nuts.

Whenever they stop for gas they call home and find out their sister has been in a hospital under sedation, but then she was taken away and no one would say by whom.

CUT TO:

INT. CALIFORNIA HOSPITAL - NEXT DAY

Once in the town in California where Chris lived, Jake, Elwood and Lamar's first stop is to pay the doctor a visit at the hospital. They track down the doctor that treated their sister and grab him, pushing him against the wall.

> **JAKE**
> Hold him against the wall and block the air from his lungs. I bet he'll find a way to tell us something!

It turned out that the doctor would say nothing and their intention is not to kill him. On the way out, an orderly walks by them and slips Jake a note. The note reads:

> **The FBI took your girlfriend and I don't know why. Don't trust anyone here.**

Jake puts the note in his pocket and stomps out to the car. Now it is time to find out about Chris. At the police station, the police will tell them nothing, other than his death is under investigation. On their way out, the desk sergeant tells them about Roxanne's car and they go to the impound lot and manage to squeeze through the hole in the fence. They find the car and see the damage the looters have done.

They walk up and down the alley several times until suddenly Jake stops. He looks at Elwood and Lamar leaning between them.

                    JAKE
    One of you better go get the car.

                    LAMAR
    I will.

Both brothers know that Jake has noticed something. As Lamar pulls the car down into the alley, Jake points to a piece of a blouse sticking out of a pile of trash.

                    JAKE
    You see that? I gave that to Roxanne for her
    eighteenth birthday and next to it is the
    bag her mom and dad gave her. She would
    never have let go of them.

As the car stops they also find a computer tower in the pile with the words… "Property of Levi" etched on the side. They remember Chris talking about his friend Levi. All the stuff goes into the back seat of the car as Jake holds the blouse up to his face.

                    JAKE
    I can still smell her.

They are really upset about what they have found, and as their long day is ending, they have two more things left to do. First they go to a bus station and put all the goods in a storage locker, and then they go to a pawn shop and buy a used computer tower.

CUT TO:

INT. RICK'S HOME - MONDAY NIGHT

Late that Monday night, Janet and her daughter check the house for more listening devices. They find that they are able to talk down in the basement, if they whisper. So it is there that they have a good cry and go to sleep on the floor.

About four o'clock in the morning Janet gets up. She wakes up Katy and they shower and dress, getting ready to leave. They gather their things, allowing only one bag each.

                              JANET
                    (Whispers to her daughter)
          Don't worry Honey; we'll get whatever else
          we need once we get on the road.

Janet carefully dismantles a section of the basement stairs, pulling out a panel. She slides out an old 1950's style black valise. It's old, square, with rusty hinges and full of documents and pictures. She slips it inside a new vinyl suitcase with wheels and a handle and takes it upstairs. She then gets several large empty trunks, some big boxes, several duffle bags and suitcases, filling some of them with only pillows. They wait by the front door.

At six o'clock sharp, the sun is just peaking over the roof tops and traffic is heavy with everyone racing to work. Just as Janet thought, the black car is still sitting down the street. Then all of a sudden there is a yellow cab in front of Janet's house.

Then there are two, and then three. The first cab pulls up and the guy gets out and comes in and grabs a big trunk, a duffle bag, takes Katy and off they go.

The second and third do the same. This is all happening in seconds. The man in the black car is frantically on the phone calling for backup. A fourth cab comes and its driver also gets some of the luggage and he takes off. More cabs keep coming, loading and leaving. The next thing you know, Janet has disappeared.

She's in one of the trunks that one of cab drivers left with. The FBI agent doesn't know what to do or which cab to follow since there must have been twenty of them coming and going, all taking some of the luggage. Within minutes the cabs have dispersed all over the city and no one knows where Janet and her daughter actually are.

CUT TO:

EXT. RICK'S NEIGHBORHOOD - DAY

Jake, Elwood and Lamar are able to piece together some of what has happened from friends, television and newspaper reports. They are now hot on a trail that is leading them to Rick's house. As they turn the corner to drive down his street, they spot the FBI's car watching his house, so they drive on by.

Then they return and slow down as they approach the black FBI car from the rear. Pulling alongside the car, Elwood, on the passenger side, rolls down his window and smiles at the agent.

The agent, thinking that they must be lost, rolls down his window and asks…

AGENT
Are you lost?

ELWOOD
No sir. We're looking for our sister and we think you boys got her some place. How about we make a trade?

Elwood holds up the counterfeit computer with Levi's name written on the side. The agent reveals his true thoughts with widening eyes.

AGENT
We don't make deals with terrorists!

They are surprised to hear that word used with regards to their family, but they know these men have information on their sister. Jake turns on his radio jammer and the FBI's car radio starts squealing. The driver looks puzzled and quickly turns it down.

ELWOOD
(Smiles, tilts his head)
You can deal with me now, or you can deal with me later. But you will deal.

Then Jake revs the motor of his fast car, spins the tires over for a short burst.

JAKE
Let's see what you boys are made of here in this fine state of California.

Jake races down to the end of the street and the chase is on. Up and down streets and hills, through people's yards until a squad car spots Jake racing by and also gives chase with the FBI following. Neither car can call for help.

After some time of fun, Jake announces that its time. He takes a sharp hairpin turn that heads up a steep hill and flips on one of his switches. A spray of black oil is pumped out the back of his car coating the road on that turn.

The squad car behind him hits the turn with all of his power and proceeds to slide off the road stopping in the top of a tree growing on the side of the hill.

Jake stops the car to make sure the police officer is okay. Then they wait for the FBI car. It slows for the curve, because they see the squad car in the trees. It stops just before the oil slick and the agents look out to see the three boys from Kentucky leaning on their car, arms crossed.

Jake, Lamar and Elwood casually get back in their car in spite of the agents waving their guns and warning that they will shoot, and slowly drive off to wait for them to figure out how to get past the oil slick.

Finally, the G-men figure out that if they drive on the grass on the other side of the road they can get by and the chase is back on. They go far up into the hills and the turns get tighter.

Fearing the guys will get away, the agent in the passenger's seat yells at the driver to keep up and he pushes the car to its limits. Then it happens. On one of the hairpin turns, Jake has stopped the car, blocking the road and the only path is over a brick wall.

The agent hits his brakes and deliberately tries to swing the car around sideways to keep from going over the wall. But the car does a donut and ends up on top of the wall, precariously balanced. The two inside are paralyzed in fear because the car is teetering on the ledge almost falling over the side.

Jake, Elwood and Lamar slowly get out of their car. Elwood sets the computer on the hood and all three guys' line up together leaning on their car, arms folded. They stand there for a moment, just surveying the predicament and then walk slowly over to the FBI car.

The two agents reach for their guns and the car starts to rock. Elwood in the center smiles and tilts his head to one side.

ELWOOD
Now that ain't very friendly. Three good law abiding citizens stop by an accident to help, and you two pull your guns. That ain't nice!

JAKE
(Smiles)
I bet one gun blast in our direction would be enough to push this fine government car right over the side, doing a lotta damage to private property. That wouldn't be good for your reputations, now would it boys?

LAMAR
(Walks forward)
Here, let me help.

He opens the passenger door and begins to gently raise and lower it. This rocks the car back and forth on the wall, causing small stones to break away.

LAMAR
Say, this ain't very stable. We had better stand back, just in case it goes over the side. We don't want anyone to get hurt.

ELWOOD
You see, you have something we want and we have something you want. Now if you don't want to play, we can just take our marbles home and try someone new another day. It's all up to you.

The agents' guns are still drawn, but now pointed up in the air.

AGENT
I told you, we don't negotiate with terrorists. That comes from the top. You're either with us or you're with them!

Lamar, still holding the door gently lifting and lowering, looks at Elwood and Jake.

LAMAR
I can't make up my mind; you guys want a burger or pizza for lunch?

JAKE
(Smiles)
Burger!

With that Lamar slowly lifts the door higher and higher until it is as high as he can lift it and the other two help give it a push over the side. It rolls down the rocky hillside and bursts into flames as it hits the bottom. Lamar looks at the other two as he dusts off his hands.

LAMAR
I didn't need your help!

ELWOOD

You didn't think I was going to let you take all the glory, do ya? I ain't going back to Pa and letting you get *all* the credit.

JAKE

That's right Lamar. We are all in this together!

LAMAR

Well you git to drive the car and Elwood gets to hold the computer. So it's only fitten I git to do *something*.

JAKE

I would let you drive, but you're nuts, Lamar.

ELWOOD

We better git goin.

JAKE

Yeah, it's time we wash this car and get something to eat. I had prepared for this type of situation and painted my car with white water-color paint so all I have to do is drive through a car wash for it to become a black car. As long as it didn't rain, we were fine.

They head back to civilization looking for a burger.

END SCENE

INT. PRISON CELL - DAY

When she first awoke and the morphine wore off, Roxanne found that she was naked and chained to a table top in a cold dark room.

At first she thought she was in an insane asylum and these people were there to help her. She tried to assure them that she was no threat to them or herself and did she not need to be restrained.

All she could envision was her brother Chris falling just out of her reach and she was full of guilt for not checking him. When she would ask of his condition, they would never answer.

It wasn't long before she found out her helpers were in fact her captors and they had other plans. She would never admit to any knowledge of or any involvement in a plan to bring down the government. This went on for days and they worked in shifts to wear her down. Roxanne's tormentors grew tired of her denying her involvement in this crime.

The old brown paint on the walls in her windowless cell was blistering and peeling off, revealing yellow water- stained plaster beneath, but not revealing its location.

As she laid there hoping someone would come to rescue her, she tried to figure out where she was. It helped to take her mind off the pain. By this time she was making up any story she could think of to make them stop torturing her.

                    ROXANNE
     Where is my brother, Chris? Is he ok? Please
     tell me if he is ok!

They would only offer to trade her information about Chris for information about their involvement in terrorism. But Roxanne had nothing to trade. The room grew colder and she was now trembling uncontrollably, chilled to the bone and terrified for she was chained to the table, as though one would need chains to hold down someone of her size.

For days now she laid shivering in her own waste, enduring torment. The only source of light was from a single bulb hanging from the ceiling in the hallway. She could hear people outside in the hall laughing. She had no more tears to cry.

When total fear was replaced with deliriousness and she had no more strength to even shiver, Roxanne began reliving her short life. Events of her past came forth from her memory. Her birthdays, her first bike, each of her dolls, each Christmas, the swimming hole where she cut her head and spent so much fun times with her brothers and their friends. She started talking to her mother and father as though they were in the room with her. Then she spoke of Jake, the man she loved with all her heart.

Outside the cell, Agents, sure that they were on to something new from all of Roxanne's babblings, fresh C.I.A. experts were brought in from Guantanamo Bay.

It was their idea to introduce her to electrical shock, a sure known way to loosen tongues. Martin told the CIA torture experts how important this was and that they had to get something out of her. They assured him the same electric shock used on those men in Cuba and Istanbul was the same they would use. Stating that "A minute or two of this will have her singing like a canary."

They hooked the heavy clamps to her arms and legs and turned on the machine. The voltage caused her body to tense rigidly. She bit down so hard in pain she bit off the tip of her tongue. The voltage was so high it began cracking her teeth.

Blood and saliva drained from her mouth as her eyes almost popped out of her head. She stared straight up at the ceiling fixed on one spot. The smell of her burning flesh filled the room as the electric contacts ate into her skin.

Over the past days her wrists and ankles were raw and bleeding from the restraints, but now the shackles cut deeply into her flesh as she twitched and stretched with all her strength. After two minutes of being on this new C.I.A. Information Extractor, they turned it off.

There was not a sound to be heard. All eyes were on Roxanne in anticipation of her finally revealing information about the terrorist cell she was believed to be a member of. Staring up at the stained ceiling, Roxanne became less rigid with pain and deep from within her came a soft gurgling sound as she let out her last agonizing breath. And so it was, after days of no sleep and little food or water, Roxanne's little body gave up the ghost, and her torment ended, all while Jake and her brothers sought to rescue her.

MARTIN
We need to keep her on ice and say nothing.
Let's let this all cool down. The more time
that passes the better.

CUT TO:

INT. MANUFACTURING PLANT - DAY

Jake, Lamar and Elwood drive off looking for food and a car wash. On their way back to civilization, they pass a large manufacturing plant set back in the hills behind a double chain link fence, with guards and guard dogs. Only the top of the building can be seen from the road. The camera focuses on it and gets closer and closer, until we see 2 men talking.

The supervisor, Jack of the armament manufacturing company is yelling at one of his engineers…

> **JACK**
> Why do we need to involve Mexico?

> **ENGINEER**
> Because, they are already aware of what we are doing and have been calling us, asking about the project. You know they're doing their own drilling and engineering. They don't want their cities leveled because the United States is not involving them.

> **JACK**
> So, are they saying that they are going to drill and detonate themselves before we do?

> **ENGINEER**
> Possibly; and that could be catastrophic. We're going to have to work with them on the same fault line. You can't just take care of one part without taking care of the other, because it's one continuous fault!

> **JACK**
> (Curtly)
> I guess you don't get it. We are a company and we have investors to think of. We gave those Mexicans a bid to do the job and they chose to have their own company do it. We are in competition with them and we don't give away trade secrets so you tell them anything you want, except the truth.

At this point Jack reports his suspicions to the F.B.I. and this engineer is picked up in the parking lot and taken away never to be seen again.

CUT TO:

INT. TELEVISION - DAY

On the television, we watch as a Presidential announcement comes on.

                    PRESIDENT
        Under my leadership, the country has been working diligently to resolve the issues of catastrophic claims in the insurance industry. I have a plan to potentially save tens of millions of dollars for the insurance companies in addition to saving lives.

After the special news report, his approval rating increases and his popularity stops sinking and starts to grow, as more and more people begin to talk about the *Reverse Wave Absorption* thing. The President is very pleased. This is what he wants, to be popular, for there is a big election coming up and he must win, at any cost. He proudly tells everyone within his circle of power just what he has done for them.

                    PRESIDENT
        When you get re-elected, it's because of me! I have saved the party and now we should have no trouble taking over.

END SCENE

INT. DINER - 6 WEEKS LATER (EVENING)

An old pickup travels down a winding road in Montana. The sun is about to set as the truck pulls into a small town, population 312, set in the foothills of the mountains where people are friendly and the air is clean. The truck stops in front of a little diner on the edge of town. It's the last building in a row of six old wooden structures. The passenger inside gets out grabs a bag out of the back, turns and thanks the driver for the ride.

The truck drives off as the diner turns on its lights for the evening. The traveler stands on the side of the road looking around taking in the crisp air and the cool night sky that is fast losing its light and filling with stars.

There are two cars parked in front and the traveler looks inside the diner window to see a waitress cleaning tables and joking with the patrons. He stands there transfixed by what he sees, his eyes taking in every movement of this woman.

His teeth clamp down hard, his abs begin to flex involuntarily and emotions well up inside. His feelings are out of control as tears begin to stream down his face. Trying to compose himself, he looks around to see if anyone is watching him. He sees no one. He decides it's better if he waits someplace else and picks a spot under a tree across the street, where he collects himself and thinks, "Can this be true?"

There is a cool breeze coming off the mountains and it helps to keep the mosquitoes at bay. There in the dark, he tries to relax but his mind races as he watches the diner intently. He realizes how he must look and can't remember how long it's been since he's had a bath. He rubs his chin and pulls at his newly grown beard, thinking "I must make quite a sight."

Finally, the last of the diner's customers leaves and they close. The lights go off and the waitress and the cook come out and lock up. They walk off together. Then a half block down they say good night and head in opposite directions.

The traveler follows the waitress a short distance to a residential area of dark streets and old homes. Suddenly, she turns down a side street and disappears. He walks a little faster trying to determine if he has missed her stepping into one of the driveways lining the shadowy street.

Its then he becomes acutely aware that he has been made. He stops in his tracks, silent, with only the sounds of muted voices and dishes being washed coming from a nearby open window.

He strains, listening for any female voice, but the next noise he hears is the sound of a revolver cocking just behind his head. No one speaks, as the two stand paralyzed in the dark with only tension filling the cool mountain air between them. The only sound now is the traveler's beating heart.

The waitress holds her gun a breath away as the hairs raise on the back of the man's neck. She quickly picks up the scent of the one who's been following her and even in his condition and in the darkness, she knows who he is. Her hands begin to tremble as her eyes fill with tears, and deep from within her soul a long guttural sound slowly begins to emerge.

Unable to hold it back, it quietly erupts as the traveler turns and sees his would be assailant. For the first time in nearly two months, Rick looks into Janet's eyes. They share a long, tight, well deserved embrace. At last, Rick asks…

RICK
Is Katy okay?

JANET
Yes, she is with a sitter. Let me get her home and to sleep, then you can come. We'll get you cleaned up first.

The next day Janet calls in sick at the diner and she, her husband and their daughter spend hours talking, laughing, and making plans. They decide to leave soon and go to Janet's parents, who live nearby on a Native American reservation about as far away from the government as you can get. Safe there, they will help care for her aging grandfather who is a decorated WWII survivor.

Her grandfather and other members of his tribe volunteered during the war, because they believed this was their country too. They were all sent to the South Pacific to serve as radiomen. Their language was only known to themselves so they could speak in their native tongue giving secret coded reports back and forth from island to island. Janet's grandfather was caught and tortured by the Japanese. He was unable to reveal what they wanted to know, because he himself didn't even know the meaning of the coded words he was sending.

CUT TO:

EXT. INDIAN RESERVATION - DAY

So one very cold day they dragged him from the barracks and made him stand barefoot on the ice as they poured water on him.

Still, he could not tell them what they wanted. After hours of standing there, he had to be ripped from the spot leaving the soles of his feet frozen to the earth.

Janet, Rick and Katy arrive on the reservation around midday and drive out to her parent's house. Only a mud path leads to the house, the only one for miles around and a dirty old car sits alongside it. The car is rusty and its tires are long gone. The house is surrounded with thigh-high green grass softly blowing in the wind. Little Katy is scared to get out of the car for the grass is over her head. She had been through a lot and it doesn't take much to set her off crying.

The small one-story house was once painted white with bright green trim and a black tar roof, as simple as it can get. Now the paint is drab and peeling off. It is easy to see all the disrepair that accompanies the old.

Mom and Dad come out to greet them with all smiles. Janet carries little Katy over to the porch with Rick in tow for them to meet him for the first time. All eyes are filled with tears of joy. As never before, Rick can see just how much Native American blood is in Janet. As they walk up the small wooden steps to enter the house.

JANET
By the way, don't call me Janet here.

The interior floor and walls are bare unpainted wooden planks about the same color as the dirt outside. In the center of this combined kitchen, dining and living room is a single plain table. Everything smells like an old cabin, but to Rick and Janet it looks like a castle. They squeeze each other's hands and smile happily, each knowing they are now safe. A voice from a back room booms out…

GRANDFATHER
Is that my Javanti ('Victorious'), whose voice I hear?

JANET
(Smiling as she looks toward her grandfather's bedroom)
Yes, and I have Raman ('Beloved') with me.

By now Katy has stopped crying and is mesmerized by the all Indian artwork hanging on the walls. She gets excited when she hears Great-grandpa's voice.

Janet walks into his room still carrying Katy in her arms. Proudly she looks at him holding her treasure. He sits up in bed and holds out his arms to take them both in. Neither seems to mind his leathery face and hands touching them. Sitting together, everyone could not stop smiling with happiness.

GRANDFATHER
Whenever you come here I tell you both I am full of new energy.
(Turning to Katy)
Ayasha ('Little One'), I had a dream about you. Your sister came to me and said to tell you not to worry about her anymore. She is with our people and she is happy and secure.

At first Rick is upset when he hears him say that and jumps up from his chair. But remembering that he is a guest and seeing how it seems to help Katy, he says nothing. He just stands in the doorway and listens. Katy has a million questions about her sister and is opening up for the first time, chattering away.

RICK (V.O.)
(Thinking)
How can that be a bad thing?

After a time, Janet's mom and dad join Rick in the doorway and their faces are full of smiles as they watch. When Katy finishes with all her questions, her worries about her sister seem to go away. The room begins takes on a new cheerfulness. Great-grandpa also has more color and a new look about him.

DAUGHTER
I am hungry, Daughter! Will you please make me some eggs and toast? There is much to do.

Grandfather had not been out of bed much for weeks, but something is now driving him. When he finishes eating, he tells them of his dreams and the urgency of his mission, leaving out many of the details.

Soon, Great-grandpa takes Katy to meet other children her age on the reservation and she begins to quickly learn their ways. The elders set up a meeting in the "round house" and all are invited, even Rick.

Members of other nearby tribes also show up for the gathering. They too have much of the same vision. The fire in the center of the round room is required to be burning twenty four hours per day, so the room is very warm. One person is endowed with the responsibility of tending the fire.

There is a long ceremony and then they get down to business as the elders speak of the end of their sacred land. They talk about how the spirits have warned them of much destruction and how they must leave the land they love. The room is filled with much sorrow, but all are resolved to do what they must to comply with the spirits' direction. Plans are made to move everyone that will go, while some of the older ones who can't make the trip would rather stay behind and die on their own land.

They map out the journey they must travel. Great-grandpa tells them they must go through the land where there are no trees. It is far to the north and will require all to help.

FLASH BACK TO WASHINGTON, DC - SECURITY COURT

It is about this same time that Martin convinces the security court that his actions are justified in the death of Roxanne as part of doing the government's business in today's times. Her side would never be told, as is the case in secret court. Martin is revered as a hero. Also, they find no need for an investigation in the deaths of Levi and Chris.

Rick and Janet remain on the FBI's missing list and the death of the two agents is written off as accidental, dying in the line of duty.

END SCENE

INT. THE GENERAL STORE - DAY

We see a delivery truck in a small town in Iowa, delivering a package to the general store of an Amish community, a place which is center to the activities of this close knit group of people.

Inside, the old wooden floors are worn from many years of those coming in for their wares. A local man makes boots and sells them there. One can buy bolts of cloth and plain buttons for their clothes. From storybooks and galvanized buckets, elixirs of all kinds to livestock treatments, it's all in the community general store. Everything is uncomplicated here and everyone is plain and modest.

The storekeeper's daughter peeks out from behind the counter. She is wearing a simple handmade grey dress with small white flowers. Her dark hair is in braids and she is barefoot. She smiles up at her father who knows what she wants. Her smile is crooked and she has trouble walking. Years of inbreeding has often left the children of this little sect with countless birth defects.

He smiles down lovingly and nods that it's okay. She limps over to the mail slot and holds the large envelope close to her as though to give it a hug. Without saying a word, she looks up at her father and gives him the biggest grin she can muster. The envelope is almost as big as she is.

One of the store's patrons notices the envelope and tells the storekeeper he will be going right by the farm that the letter is addressed to. They both spend a lot of time looking it over trying to determine its contents.

It has traveled a long distance, all the way from California. The storekeeper is also the postmaster of their community. He tells the patron that someone at the farm must sign the green card and return it to him, and then he shows him where to have it signed. Thus, the large envelope travels safely on, resting on the front seat of the old Amish buggy, slowly being pulled down a gravel road by a single horse.

Cars race by like much of time has, but eventually the envelope arrives intact at its destination. The man takes the letter to the back door of the designated farmhouse and is greeted by Levi's mother and his little sister and brother. All are clean and barefoot, but the plague of their community is in this home as well. The letter is addressed to Levi and his mother will not touch it. She sends the boy to call her husband in from the field. When he races in, even he has trouble getting near it. He is a big muscular man. The years of working a farm show in his hands and face.

After some time, and discussing it with his trusted friend, he is convinced it is safe and he signs the green card with a slow and deliberate signature. The whole family gathers around the kitchen table and stands motionless, watching in anticipation.

The room is spotless, from the white walls to the daily scrubbed wooden floor. The floor is so clean you could literally eat off it. Also in the kitchen is an old wood burning stove that is bigger than the table. It too is so clean it looks brand new, not a hundred years old. Next to it is one of those galvanized buckets from the general store full of husked corn.

The room is warm from the stove that is always burning. The father opens the envelope very carefully as to do no damage. The gentleness by which he handles it is clear to all and it's out of respect for his son. Inside is a letter from a patent attorney in California.

LEVI'S MOTHER
(Screams)
STOP!!!! READ NO MORE!!!! HE IS DEAD, MY SON IS DEAD!!!!! THEY HAVE KILLED HIM!!!

PATENT OFFICE LETTER
I have sent you several letters and you have not responded. Therefore, I have taken the liberty of sending the enclosed information to your parents' home address. Please find attached the original United States of America Patent number 5,366,463 registered in your name. I hope this finds its way safely to your hands.…

Levi's mother runs to the corner of the room holding her children's ears to protect them from the letter.

LEVI'S MOM
GET IT OUT OF OUR HOUSE!!

Levi's father, Zachariah, complies with her request and they take the letter outside. There he gives it back to his neighbor.

ZACHARIAH
This is something we may need to discuss in the church meeting this Sunday. We know nothing of these things.

                        NEIGHBOR
    Maybe we should ask preacher Benson. He is
    one of the outsiders and may know what to
    do.

                        ZACHARIAH
         (Somberly)
    Yes, ask him if he will come.

Word spreads fast in their community and by Sunday everyone knows about the letter. Emotions are all across the board. Some want the whole family to be shunned from their church, but others are not so mean spirited. No one speaks openly of it until this day.

On Sunday meeting day, the horse drawn carts and wagons slowly pull up to the small wooden church, built almost one hundred years ago. So as not to offend his friends, Preacher Benson arrives with neighbors in one of the finest buggies. He is considered an honored guest. Everyone politely greets him and slowly moves into the church to sit down on the old wooden pews.

People are polite but not friendly to Zachariah. The seats are all facing the center of the room, where there is a large wood burning stove. Like Levi's home, this place too is spotless. Services in the past have sometimes been known to be very quiet. Anyone can speak up when the Lord so inspires them.

Today all settle in to enjoy the solemnity, but Zachariah is looking around the room into the eyes of each of his neighbors. Preacher Benson sits next to Zachariah and his wife when they all first came in. He knows it is a great honor to be asked to come and give homage to the Lord. Fearing no one will bring up the reason he was invited, he stands up and gives thanks to God for all their blessings and then turns to Zachariah's neighbor and asks to see the letter.

                        WOMAN
    You brought this thing sent from Satan's
    hands into God's house!

                        MAN
    The whole family should be shunned!

Preacher Benson raises his arms in an attempt to bring calmness into the room.

PREACHER BENSON

Who are we to bring anger into God's house? This is a time to discuss things respectfully. We should leave our anger outside. What is it that a piece of paper can make you turn against each other? Let me see this letter.

He turns to Zachariah, who has not said a word and holds out his hand. Zachariah looks over at the woman that first yelled out.

ZACHARIAH

The letter is outside in the buggy. I did not want him to bring it inside either, until all agreed.

With that, the woman looks down and apologizes.

NEIGHBOR

They did not want it in their house and I understand. We don't want it in ours either, but they need our help and guidance. I for one am going to give that help to one of my neighbors.

He then walks out to the buggy and returns with the letter.

LEVI'S MOTHER
(Loudly)
COVER THE CHILDREN'S EARS!

All the women comply.

Preacher Benson stands up, takes the letter and reads it to himself.

PREACHER BENSON

This is not a bad thing. Your son did something wonderful.

MAN
(Standing up and shaking his fist at Benson)
That cannot be true! We saw the black car come to your home with the government men inside. You, along with your son, brought them into our community. He has dreams of doing great things. Vanity runs (more)

through his veins and now it has brought his poison to us all.

Zachariah stares hard at the man, slowly rises to his feet and clenches his powerful fist.

> **MAN #2**
> (Jumps to his feet and blurts out)
> He is right. Levi is always doing the work of the devil. He reads those books all the time and his head is filled with delusions of grandeur. Like I've said before, only evil could come of this.

> **PREACHER BENSON**
> (Pointing at man #2)
> The word of God comes to you from such a book. Are you telling all of us this book is also bad?

The man quietly sits back down.

> **LEVI'S MOTHER**
> (Standing)
> I told them not to bring it into our house and I don't want this evil in here now. This is God's house! It's not a place for work from the hand of the devil!

> **PREACHER BENSON**
> (Smiling)
> What better place? Let's all hold any evil up to the light of God for us all to see. Then we will know the right path to take.

Preacher Benson holds up the patent and shows off its red ribbon and large gold seal for everyone to see.

> **PREACHER BENSON**
> This is what you are granted when you have a new and bright idea that no one else has ever thought of before. The federal government has issued such a patent to your son Levi and...

> **ELDER**
> (Standing and yells)
> STOP RIGHT THERE!! There is the proof you seek! He said it with those words. We all know the government is not to be (more)

trusted and now they have found their way here. You and your whole family should be shunned from our community.

Preacher Benson is about to speak, when an old man in the back pounds his cane on the railing. All know him to be the oldest member of their community, and his word is highly respected. It is hard for him to stand for the years are heavy on his back. His family is there to help him up to his feet and they stand next to him as though his words speak for them all. They are one.

                ELDEST ELDER
(Clears his throat)
I can't believe what I am hearing. Some of you are right. Satan is here in this room today, but evil was not brought here in the form of a letter, but in the poison in your own hearts. I have lived long enough to remember Zachariah's father and grandfather. I know this family to be good god-fearing people and so do all of you.
    Levi was always a good boy and first in line to help anyone. There is not a person in this room that has not felt the hands of love and friendship from these people on their farms and in their homes.
    Now you turn against them when they need your help the most. Look not to the devil from the outside, but look for the beast that has gotten into your souls. That is the only devil I see in this room.

The elder then looks down and the years clearly show on his sad face. No one speaks, for he is still standing, and it's clear he is not finished. He looks back up and turns his head back and forth looking for someone.

                ELDEST ELDER
Where is Sarah? You all know my great granddaughter. She had the twisted foot and could barely walk when she was little. Levi helped her with therapy and a leg brace he made from reading one of those books you all have been talking about. Today she walks pretty well.
(He points to the center of the room)
Walk on out there and show them Sarah.

Sarah hides behind her mother's dress holding on for dear life and peeks out. With encouragement from the family she finally comes out and walks to the center of the room.

> ELDEST ELDER
> That's what Levi did. You all know he wanted to become a doctor and help people. Now Sarah has something to say. Go on and tell them.

Sarah turns red and looks down at her feet.

> ELDEST ELDER
> Ok I will start… Sarah had a dream two nights ago. Levi came to check on her… alright, you finish it Sarah.

Sarah bravely looks up and at everyone in the room.

> SARAH
> He checked my leg. He was all white and he came with my grandma. She sat on my bed next to me and told me many people loved me. After Levi looked at my leg, he looked up at me and said his work was done. He said that I was all cured and did not need to wear the brace anymore. Grandma said they were both in heaven and he wanted me to tell you all that he was loved and in a safe place. Not to worry and get on with your lives.

At this point Levi's mother breaks down.

> LEVI'S MOTHER
> I told you that he was dead. How do I bury my son when we don't have him here?

Suddenly all the poison that had seemed to fill the room was gone and people were going to her to comfort her. She is sobbing uncontrollably.

> PREACHER BENSON
> (Putting his hand on Zachariah's shoulder)
> Now, we really don't know if he is dead or not, but why don't we get together next week and have a ceremony in his honor? We can all write memories of all his good deeds and place them in a pine box with the (more)

> patent letter and bury it in the family plot on your land.

Everyone likes that idea and so it was planned that at the next prayer meeting, that was exactly what they would do. There is a corner of every farm that is designated as the family cemetery and it is their custom to bury the dead standing up so as to take up less space. Levi's small pine box was to hold a place of high honor in his family's plot.

CUT TO:

EXT. THE RESERVATION - DAY

At about the same time as the meeting at the Amish Community was taking place; Rick and Janet were helping the families on the reservation who wanted to leave, heeding the warnings. Few remained behind.

Like a wagon train heading to a new promised land, they head out where arrangements are made for their arrival on another reservation near Glacier Bay. It was said to be the last northern rain forest in the world. The federal government had licensed the timber industry to harvest all the trees, grind them into pulp and ship it overseas. They would become the voice of this land.

CUT TO:

EXT. RAILROAD STATION, KENTUKY - DAY

Simultaneously, Chris's body has finally been released by the federal government. The family has to pay to have him and his things shipped back home to Kentucky. He arrives unceremoniously by train in a crate. Jake, Elwood and Lamar are the only ones there to greet him. They slide his coffin and his belongings into the back of their pick-up. It was time to bring him home.

Afterwards, Jake stands on the loading dock and watches the train slowly move away. A single tear runs down his cheek.

          JAKE
Now we only need one more.

          LAMAR
    (Gently puts his large hand on
    Jakes shoulder and says softly)
We will get her or we will get even.

Elwood too is watching the train and he turns to Jake…

                              ELWOOD
            From the start we all knew you and Roxanne
            were meant to be. You are a part of our
            family now. You drive the truck.

Elwood and Lamar ride in the back with their brother. Jake keeps the old truck in first gear while he slowly drives down Main Street. The whole town pauses. People come out of stores and line up to pay tribute to Chris and to their family. They all mistrust the government and this just fuels their anger.

Word travels quickly and soon the whole town knows Chris is back. As the truck pulls onto the property of Chris's family a light mist begins to fall. They notice the yard is full of cars and trucks from all over. The whole family has turned out for this moment.

Jake can see that everyone has gathered in the barn to stay dry and he gradually pulls the truck through the big double doors. No one says a word as they get out of the truck. They all stand silently staring at the crate in the back. Then Ma breaks down and so do the others.

                                PA
                     (Walking over to the truck)
            Did you check it?

                              LAMAR
                     (Looking at the crate)
            No sir, we did not feel it was right to open
            it without you.

                                PA
            Open it.

They grab two crowbars and pry the lid up. All four stand on the back of the truck and look down. The smell was gagging, but they did not flinch. Their eyes widen as they look in trying to identify him. Pa looks at Lamar, the oldest of his boys and softly asks…

                                PA
            Is it him?

Lamar's eyes are still moving over the body of his brother who appears to have been haphazardly tossed in like he was trash. The head injuries, the bruising and swelling make it next to impossible to tell who it is. Then Lamar raises Chris's left pant leg to reveal three small round scars.

                              LAMAR
          It's him Pa. That's where he fell on that
          pitch fork when we was kids jumping out of
          the barn window into the hay.

                               PA
          Close it. I don't want the others to see
          what they've done to him.

A voice in the back yells out…

                          CHRIS' UNCLE
          Like hell, he was my nephew and I loved him
          as much as you. You keep it open Lamar and
          get out of my way. I want to see what those
          bastards did.

Soon everyone climbs up into the back of the truck, even Ma. It seems to suck the life out of her. More people begin to show up to pay their respects. They bring dishes of all kinds of food and offer to help in any way they can. Coming from the house you could hear the phone ringing off the hook.

                              JAKE
                (Turning to Ma)
          Do you want me to get it?

                               MA
          No, it's just those collection people
          calling for payments on Chris's and
          Roxanne's student loans. Hell, he owes five
          times what he borrowed. I can't figure out
          how they can do that. And they won't stop.

                              JAKE
          Did you tell him he was dead?

                               MA
          Yes! At least ten times. But they keep
          calling. I would turn the damn thing off if
          it weren't for Roxanne. I keep it on for
          her. We don't know, she may call one day and
          tell us she is okay.

People from Roxanne's church begin showing up to give support, even though they understand that she is still gone and most likely will come home the same way as Chris. The preacher wants to make a statement and climbs up on a bale of hay.

> **PREACHER**
> This may not be the right time, but we ask ourselves, when *will* it be the right time? Today Roxanne's whole Sunday school class wanted to be here to show you a project they have been working on. Billy, come out here and tell everyone what you have planned.

A small boy walked to the center of the barn and showed off a small box with a wire coming out of it. He held it up for all to see.

> **BILLY**
> Well it's not really my idea, it's my brother's. He came back from Iraq, where they blew him up. He lost both his legs and part of his face. He remembers Roxanne and your family and he wanted to share his plan, which he calls *Roxanne's Revenge*.
>
> There is a place not far from here, where the federal government has set up big devices to listen to outer space for space aliens. He said they can spend hundreds of millions on that while we have homeless people going hungry. Well anyway, it just infuriates him, so he made this thing, a radar beeper.
>
> The battery lasts up to a year and it puts out a signal that interrupts the government's research. He wants us to make up hundreds of these things and attach them to the backs of wild animals and release them in this area, you know, for Roxanne's revenge.

The whole place becomes hushed until finally the preacher walks up and says…

> **PREACHER**
> That was a good presentation Billy. Thank you.

Then Chris's father walks over and gets down on his knees to look at the device. He holds it in his hand and looks up at the boy.

> **PA**
> You tell your brother that I really like the idea and we thank him for thinking of (more)

us. He just needs to tell me what we can do to help get it going.

Finally, a grave is dug and Chris is buried next to the rest of the family. He was an atheist and this is how he wanted it. Soon, all the people from town leave and Chris' father speaks privately to the family.

            PA
That was a nice send-off for my boy, but this ain't where it's goin to stop, this is where it starts. It was nice of everyone to think of Roxanne like that as well. It's good to see other people stepping up and taking sides against the real enemy. But we are goin to do a lot more than sendoff radar beeps, and it's going to take all of us.

END SCENE

INT. PROJECT OFFICE - DAY

Back in California, *Project Reverse Wave Absorption* is nearing completion. Unfortunately, the program is still missing a formula regarding the exact positioning of detonations. Also, the armaments manufacturer is having a considerable amount of difficulty with some of the engineers. They have banded together and are saying this whole scheme is extremely dangerous, that the drilling and setting off bombs for hundreds of miles along a fault line is unsafe.

One claims that if you release that kind of pressure, the result could cause a free-floating plate that could slide for miles. And, there is another country to consider as well -- Mexico. They also claim that since the fault goes right through Mexico City, the Mexican government must be consulted. Finally, Jack has had it with them and asks them to leave the project, telling them their services are no longer needed.

The contractors finish developing the drilling machines to set the bombs deep in the earth, and the plan is underway. The bombs are made, the holes are drilled and the money flows. But, Levi's model includes another unresolved problem. That is, if all this pressure is released at one time, what would the *global* effect be? Keeping this in mind, Levi's plan stresses the importance of maintaining strictly isolated, yet sequential, detonations for the purpose of pulverizing the rock between two shifting plates.

However, the armament contractors have designed for too many detonation sites with explosives way too big and over too long of distances. This is totally against the protocol that Levi's engineering program outlines; all of which has been updated and included on the computer that Chris was fixing when he died. The bottom line is that Jack doesn't care about getting the job done right, he just wants to make more money and more bombs mean more money.

Also on Levi's real computer are his calculations in his engineering format which had been a real breakthrough for him. They show how to use minimal explosives in intervals, and you reverse the wave for many short distances. What happens is that the fissure is disrupted at the very tip so that any *one* explosion doesn't disrupt the entire earthquake. When the earthquake does happen on its own, the plate will already have been pulverized in just the areas under highly populated locations where there is greatest concern, not the entire fissure.

Therefore, when the plates move and the earthquake happens, it will be a *controlled* event, causing very little damage to designated cities. In the eventuality that it doesn't activate a major earthquake as he predicts, when the big one does come, every city down that is on the fault line will have had the stressed areas pulverized. The pulverized granite will allow for a smooth slide, and the buildings above won't snap and crumble. The underground plates will just slide by each other effortlessly, which is the whole purpose of *Reverse Wave Absorption*.

On the other hand, there is a calculation on Levi's real computer showing the extreme dangers of creating a free-floating plate with explosions that are too large. If the release of pressure is overdone, it could cause other nearby plates to move and affect others all around the world, inadvertently. Unfortunately, Levi's computer, along with this crucial information, is now in Chris's bedroom in Kentucky amongst Chris's other belongings that were sent on the train with his body.

Nonetheless, the day of detonation finally arrives and every major city along the California coast has been evacuated within a hundred miles of the fault line. There are no major grass fires happening, weather conditions seem suitable with no hurricanes or other major storms brewing. Once the entire area is evacuated, all gas lines are turned off and everything is shut down.

The detonations are set off with remarkable precision and *Project Reverse Wave Absorption* is carried out as planned. The San Andreas Fault lines shift and because the ground between each plate is pulverized in such a fashion, they literally pass each other without major damage. Crews are sent in to inspect and repair any damaged lines and to inspect all bridges and tall buildings. Other than a few cracks in some roadways and one downed bridge, the operation is declared a complete success.

Air Force One arrives in California and the President of the United States steps off his jet with the news cameras rolling. In his news conference, he takes all the credit for this amazing operation, even as the ground beneath them rumbles and a crack emerges across the runway where he is speaking.

Within twenty four hours the last of the gas lines is being repaired. The man in the ditch yells out, "53 inches," while another man above cuts an eight inch pipe and passes it down to him. As he is setting it, he yells out…

GAS MAN
You cut it too short, I said 53 inches.

> **HELPER**
> I cut it 53 inches!

He checks the distance again and it's now 54 inches. Holding onto the pipe sticking out of the ground, he can feel it vibrating. He measures one more time and he now needs 55 inches. At this point, he climbs out and calls his supervisor.

What has happened is what those fired engineers feared, too much detonation was used and now the plate is in free-float formation. Roads begin developing new cracks every hour. California hasn't stopped moving.

CUT TO:

EXT. GLACIER BAY RESERVATION - EVENING

Meanwhile, Rick, Janet, Katy and the rest of the "wagon train" arrive safely at their new destination and their first order of business is to set up camp. By now Katy has become an official Native American Indian, and Rick has come to his own conclusion.

> **RICK** (V.O.)
> (Thinking)
> Well I tried it their way. Now I will try it this way. It's time for me to write my book and reveal the truth about the Kennedy murder.

The old black valise has made the trip safely to Glacier Bay with Janet.

CUT TO:

INT. AMISH CHURCH - DAY

Continuing to switch from scene to scene

It is the day of Levi's tribute and the small Amish church fills up with people quickly. They have come from all over to honor Levi. There are so many people in fact, some have to wait outside and take turns going in. In the center of the room sits a small white pine box on a stand and behind it, is Levi's family. They greet each person coming in one at a time, remembering the person known as Levi. Some bring flowers, others just memories and still others prepared statements and notes to go in the memory box. One young man comes in and behind him, Preacher Benson.

PREACHER BENSON
This is my son Joshua. He wishes to tell you something.

A tear runs down the young man's cheek as he tries to speak, but can hardly get the words to come out. He unfolds a piece of paper and holds it in his trembling hands. Finally he composes himself, clears his throat to speak.

JOSHUA
(Looking at all the faces in the room)
It's my fault. Levi so loved to help people. It was me who encouraged him to join me in my goal of going to college and becoming a doctor. I gave him books to read and I taught him how to use my computer. Only he was much smarter than me and he is the one that got the scholarship. It's because of me he went away and now he is gone.

He begins to sob and Zachariah and his family came over to hug him and thank him for being a friend. And so the day goes. The box fills with letters and notes. At the end the box is sealed and nailed down with square nails. It is carried out and given to Levi's mother and she holds it lovingly like a newborn baby.

A procession of carts and buggies lead the way to Zachariah's farm, where they stop on the side of the road, close to the graveyard of their family. There in the far corner of the farm field are the small white gravestones, all arranged next to one another sticking out of the ground, their points upright pointing to the heavens above. A neat freshly dug grave is waiting for Levi's box. It is the custom of the Amish bury their dead upright, so as to take up less space.

So upright is Levi's little white box, six inch by six inch and about two feet high, also being placed in the ground, and Levi's mother insists on setting the stone. Once set, it will only stick twelve inches out of the ground. The only mark on it is Levi's name, hand carved by one of the neighbors.

There is not much time to mourn, because the next day is a big day for their daughter, who is to meet her new husband coming from another Amish community in Pennsylvania. It is because of these closely related communities, there are many birth defects from inbreeding. They now exchange their eligible young women between communities, whereas there was a time when they would just pack them up and send them off. But after much ridicule from outsiders they have slowed down the process of betrothal and marriage and now permit courtship, or a pretense of courtship.

CUT TO:

EXT. CALIFORNIA - DAY

Back in California, emergency systems are in full use, because too many explosives were used by the President's company in *Project Reverse Wave*, California is still moving and things have reached emergency status. The state had been declared safe by the President and the people were welcomed back only to find the land is crumbling into the sea. Bridges are collapsing and just like what happened in Louisiana, during Hurricane Katrina, government helicopters are lifting people out of dangerous situations.

At Yellowstone National Park, the earth is moving there as well, only difference is, the direction it is moving is up. New fissures have opened and Old Faithful stopped erupting every hour and now is flowing in a constant stream. Cracks are opening all over the place in the ground. The few remaining tribe members on the reservation there have decided to go north and join their families at the new location. No one is left and the park has closed.

CUT TO:

INT. JAKE'S FAMILY HOME - DAY

Meanwhile, in Kentucky, Jake's grandfather is well known in the area because of his moonshine days. He was the best at outrunning the G-men and never got caught. The Tennessee Valley Authority took all of his parents' land for their dam projects, telling them they needed it for power plants. But it turned out that a few of the project managers kept some of the high ground with prime views of the new lakes for themselves and sold it for big profits.

Jake's family got pennies for their property and they got rich. That, and his grandfather's old stories of what the Yankees did after the civil war, is why he got into the moonshine business anyway. When he was running from the G-men, he developed a fog machine that he hooked up to his car. When they got too close, he would turn it on and lose them in a cloud of smoke every time.

He had quite a reputation and everyone respected him. One day they caught up with him and made him a deal. They would set him up in business and he would own a patent on his machine if he would build it for the government to be used on all the PT boats. As a result, Jake's grandfather became a very wealthy man.

The phone rings.

The nurse answers the phone and starts to takes a message when she realizes that it's important, she puts the phone down. She heads into Jake's Grandfather's bedroom and tells him of the call. He is now in his nineties and is still as sharp as a tack. He even drives his own car. He takes the call.

It's the jeweler that made the engagement ring for Jake that he gave to Roxanne. The jeweler asks him to have Jake stop by his store, because the ring has been found. The old man jumps of bed and yells at the nurse to find Jake and to have him get the car ready. Quickly, Jake meets him in the drive and off they go.

Jake drives and Gramps tells him the story the jeweler told him on the way and in no time they're at the store. The jeweler pulls out a small plastic bag from behind the counter and hands it to Jake. He takes the ring out of the bag as his eyes fill with tears. He lovingly strokes it, knowing that Roxanne is dead, for she would never have taken off her ring or lost track of it. The jeweler also takes out several pieces of paper.

JEWELER
I found your ring for sale on the internet. I buy a lot of my stuff that way. When I saw it come up for sale I knew instantly it was hers. I recognized my own hand work. I made that ring especially for you to give to Roxanne. Anyway, I made sure I was the top bidder.
Apparently, the ring came from South America and the buyer's information is now long gone, but I did print what I could when he was up and running. That's how these crooks operate. I never buy from people I don't know, but this ring was going to be mine, I would have made a deal with the devil to get it back.

He stopped there for a moment to give Jake time to get composed. Gramps is visibly shaken as well. Everybody had all hoped that somehow, Roxanne would be coming back into their lives, and that hope was now gone. The jeweler continues…

> **JEWELER**
> I am sorry to have to be the one to do this. I really cared for Roxanne too. I wanted to make sure before I called you, but I didn't want you waste any time either. It just arrived today, and those papers may help track down who really sold it, but you'll need to find someone better at computers than me.

There was one long deep cut in the side of the ring. Jake ran his finger over and over it as though that would help bring him closer to Roxanne. Gramps stuck out his hand to shake the jeweler's and to thank him.

> **GRAMPS**
> How much do we owe you?

> **JEWELER**
> Not a cent, sir. A man does not take money for a chance to help in a case like this. You find who did this and that will be my payment. And if you need help slitting his throat, you call me.

Jake held the small ring tight in his hand, thanked the jeweler and shook his hand as well.

> **JAKE**
> If I ever get my hands on who did this I will hold a private party and we can all can have a piece of him. I think I know who is partly responsible.

Just then the ground begins to rumble and the glass booth starts to shake. Then it stopped. Jake lets Gramps drive when they leave as he continues to hold onto Roxanne's ring. He then puts it on the chain around his neck, tucks it inside his shirt and pats his chest, thinking…

> **JAKE** (V.O.)
> Now you will always be near my heart.

When they get back home, Jake tells Gramps that he has to go, that he is running very late. Gramps tells him he wishes he could go, but they both know he is too old. Jake gets into his 'pride and joy' and checks his load. It's all secure and he is off. He arrives late at Chris' family farm, where everyone is all loaded and the caravan is just starting to head out. Chris's father stops Jake.

> **CHRIS' DAD**
> I won't stop you, but I will ask you to think about what you are about to do. You can't make me grandbabies from a prison cell.

Jake pulls out the chain from around his neck and shows him Roxanne's ring.

> **JAKE**
> I think my future is with you.

And without saying another word they get in the cars and head out. The road winds far up into the hills and when they are in the clouds they stop and unload the boxes. The entire family helped make the fake marijuana plants they carry and the hand painted cloth sewn to the wire mesh soldered to wire rods and bent in such a way that they really look very life-like.

They all check their watches for the time. It is getting close. The fake plants are all laid out in neat rows looking like they have been growing there all year. The men ask the women to leave and go back to safety, but none would have anything to do with that.

Once again the ground begins to tremble under their feet. The die is cast. The call is made and the chopper is on its way. An anonymous tip was called into the Bureau of ATF, and soon they hear their chopper growing closer and closer. Everyone is now hiding in the undergrowth with the cars, all out of sight. The chopper spots the plants and moves in for a better look.

Immediately, they all open fire, and over a thousand bullets hit the chopper as it lifts off. It seems as though nothing has happened, and then they hear it, the motor misfires, flames shoot out the back and the chopper crashes into the side of the mountain. Everyone lets out a cheer, and Chris' father climbs up on the back of his truck.

> **CHRIS' DAD**
> That one was for my boy. You all saw what they did to him. But this war is not over. Where is our Roxanne? How could they take her away from us too? We all know in our hearts that she is never coming home. I vow to never stop my vengeance. My wife and I are getting old and this war is going to have to be passed on to y'all. Now let's go get another one for our Roxanne!

No one even notices the next earth's tremor as Jake yells out to everyone to pick up the fake plants.

                      JAKE
        Make sure you don't leave anything behind.
        Let's get out of here.

END SCENE

EXT. THE DESERT - DAY

We open to a desert scene, where we see the patch of burnt ground where Chris' body was lit a fire. A desert storm blowing. At this point is our epilog. We start to see a series of scenes and our narrator describes what is taking place.

> **NARRATOR** (O.S.)
> Levi's body was never found. Instead his mother and father would morn over an empty grave on their Amish farm. A sand storm in the desert the day after he was dumped and burned by the FBI covered all evidence by four feet of sand. This made James very happy. There would be no chance of an investigation because Mother Nature had done the cover up for them. Buford's body was there too, remaining diligently at his side, in their unmarked, solitary grave.
> Roxanne's body was placed in a standard black body bag tagged, "DO NOT OPEN - TOP SECRET," and then frozen solid. It was found that this was the best way to store them until they could be disposed of, especially to hold down the smell. Several weeks later she was transported to a California Navy base. There she and others like her were taken by ship to a specific location in the Pacific Ocean, placed in a large weighted down steel cage and unceremoniously pushed over the side to sink and finally rest in the same ocean graveyard as the discarded nuclear submarines. Because this particular area is classified as a no-dive zone by the government, soon the crabs would dispose of any remains.
> Eight of Chris and Roxanne's immediate family members were convicted in absentia under the Sedition Act and remain wanted criminals. Chris and Roxanne's mother and father received the higher honor of being placed on the FBI's twenty most wanted list of home grown terrorists, as well as being found guilty of acts of sedition. It is believed they are still somewhere in the hills of Kentucky and being hidden by family and friends. A pit bull named Chopper who was sired by Buford is their constant companion and protector.

NARRATOR (O.S.)

Rick, Janet and their family lived a quiet life at Glacier Bay. A Swiss bank account held enough money to keep the reservation and everyone living there taken care of for generations. The money came from the worldwide sales of a blockbuster expose' written by a secret informant close to the Kennedy assassination cover-up. Suddenly, evidence appeared that had never been seen before. No one but Janet and James ever knew the mole was Rick. The original documents and manuscripts were anonymously turned over to the World Supreme Court in Geneva.

The President was considered a hero for his part in saving California's insurance industry billions of dollars and countless lives. Because of their corporate greed, Jack's Company used hundreds of times too many explosives to release the fault, but they also made hundreds of millions of dollars.

The President was reelected in a landslide clean sweep and the Republican Party took over the government in almost total power. Their first act of new power was to pass a new retirement plan for themselves worth millions and protected under the Security Act.

Yellowstone National Park closed soon after Rick, his family and the others left for Glacier Bay. The earth became very unstable throughout the region. New geysers formed as swelling opened up new fissures. The movement of the plates in California picked up speed reaching one foot per hour. Much of the land continued in a slow moving churning sea of rubble, slowly grinding and pushing its way from Mexico City to the Pacific Ocean. Grinding, popping and burning, the dust and smoke made it impossible to determine how bad the destruction really was. But based on what one could see, you were lucky if you weren't there and the area all along the fault lines remained uninhabitable.

Earthquake activity increased all over the planet. Dust, dirt, smoke and ash filled the air all over the earth blocking the sun and disrupting communication. In (more) fact, there was a report that a growing shelf on one of the Hawaiian Islands broke off creating a tidal wave five hundred feet high. When it crashed on shore one thousand miles away, few had time to escape. Tidal waves around the world caused catastrophic flooding in places as far away as Florida, New York, Ireland and New Zealand.

Yellowstone continued to erupt more and more as rivers were replaced with lava flows. Plumes of ash filled the air and rose into the upper atmosphere. The sun began to disappear. Very unexpectedly, there occurred what is called a super eruption and for hundreds of miles the earth opened up as ash filled the sky over Yellowstone.

The earth's sky was no longer blue but became permanently dark gray and in some places totally black as the earth went into a long winter. Hundreds of feet of ash fell on some cities entombing its people. The empowered Republican Party declared martial law when much of the United States became uninhabitable and plans were put in place to move the government officials to safer ground. Senators, congressmen, governors, mayors and even councilmen began a war. The Republicans and Democrats fought over where to relocate, as pleas went out to other countries for help, but no one would have anything to do with them. The Republicans decided to move their members of the Senate and Congress to the North Pole, and the Democrats moved to the South Pole.

The first order of business was to build brand new facilities to house them in the style they had become accustomed to. Much of the planet began drifting into a new ice age as millions starved to death.

Before long, no country would trade with the United States for their money had no value and most blamed them for the world's new problems. All U.S. political parties were put on trial by the World Supreme Court for numerous charges. They were found guilty on all charges including:

1. Placing personal gains over the welfare of those they represent and thereby killing untold millions. (more)

2. Setting up puppet governments for the oil companies.
3. War profiteering
4. Not prosecuting bankers for fraud and schemes of snatch and grab.
5. Kidnapping
6. Torture
7. Murder
8. The 1963 coup and cover-up in which President Kennedy and others were assassinated.
9. Authorizing the tobacco industry to add nicotine additives to its product, making it more addictive than cocaine.
10. Reducing toy inspections to one person allowing exposure to toxic chemicals.
11. Allowing chemical experimentation on people via the pharmaceutical industry by insufficient supervision of the FDA. And the list went on….

There was a lot of controversy over sentencing. Many countries wanted guilty politicians put to death. "Let our planet be purged of this evil!" they demanded. Soon after, the criminal political empire, known as the Republican and Democratic parties, was no more.

A single world government took over with the only goal being to insure man's continued existence in harmony with nature, the earth and all remaining life. Money was the first thing to be outlawed. Research continued in the study of genes and it took years, but a scientist discovered what became known as the Ethic Gene. It was mandatory for every human to be tested for this gene and if you were found to be lacking it, you were given two options, death or sterilization. Those not willing to be tested were executed. And as it is written, the meek inherited the earth.

www.ingramcontent.com/pod-product-compliance
Lightning Source LLC
Chambersburg PA
CBHW082356220526
45470CB00008B/2760